Individual Action Planning: A Practical Guide

Gillian Squirrell

D0061064

David Fulton Publishers

London

2 Barbon Close, London WC1N 3JX

First published in Great Britain by
David Fulton Publishers 1995

Note: The right of Gillian Squirrell to be identified as the author of this work has been asserted by her in accordance with the copyright, Designs and Patents Act 1988.

British Library Cataloguing in Publication Data

A catalogue record for this book is available from the British Library

ISBN 1-85346-253-5

Typeset by Textype Typesetters, Cambridge
Printed in Great Britain by the Cromwell Press Ltd., Melksham

Contents

Preface

This book is intended to take you through the various steps in Individual Action Planning and to assist you in helping young people devise their own Action Plans and develop their planning skills.

The book explains why Individual Action Planning (IAP) is useful to teaching, tutoring, careers and guidance staff and to young people themselves. The book sets Individual Action Planning within its broader context and makes reference to the value which IAP has to end-users, such as employers.

The book sets out to answer the questions which you might have about IAP and those which pupils, colleagues and senior managers may ask you.

The book includes examples of Individual Action Plans and supporting materials.

It is hoped that the Guide and materials will stimulate your thinking about how IAP might be used within your own teaching, guidance or training context.

Gillian Squirrell
Bristol, July 1994

Acknowledgements

This book would not have been possible without the work of many colleagues who were funded during 1989–92 by the Employment Department who were involved in developing and delivering the Youth Development Project Initiative.

1 Introduction

This book is intended for practitioners in education and training, and their colleagues in the guidance services. It is a practical text which explores Individual Action Planning and Individual Action Plans. The first part of the book reviews the various stages of the Individual Action Planning (IAP) cycle, describes the skills which are needed to negotiate each stage effectively, and considers some of the issues which arise for students and teaching staff as they work through each phase of the cycle.

The second part takes a broader view of IAP. It explores the implications of the principles which underpin Action Planning, considers the roles of the various partners in the planning cycle and describes the web of relationships which support young people most effectively through IAP.

The book offers a comprehensive overview of IAP for those new to it and to gives those to some degree already *au fait* with IAP the opportunity to explore issues in greater depth and to accumulate ideas for inservice work with colleagues.

The rest of this introductory chapter considers briefly the following fundamental questions:

- What is IAP?
- What are Individual Action Plans?
- What do they offer?
- Why use the term 'individual'?
- Where do Individual Action Plans and IAP lead?

What is Individual Action Planning and an Individual Action Plan?

IAP and Individual Action Plans are processes and documents with increasing and widespread currency in education, training, employment and guidance. Elements of IAP underpin many developments in youth and adult guidance, and form the basis of occupational appraisal. Action Planning principles can be found in schools and colleges as part of formative assessment processes and in the holistic profiling of student progress.

An Individual Action Plan can be considered as a route map assisting an individual to move from their current position to a pre-determined goal. The goal and the means to reach it having been determined through the guidance and counselling process which underpins all IAP.

IAP and an Individual Action Plan are not synonymous terms. The former is the process which leads to the product, the Action Plan. The terms cannot be interchanged, the process and the product have different functions and offer different benefits to young people and those working with them.

Individual Action Planning

IAP is a series of discussion sessions between a young person and an impartial adult. IAP sessions focus on the young person's achievements and interests, and the ways in which these might, if appropriate, be developed. The young person's aspirations (personal, vocational or educational) are discussed as is their realisation.

IAP is a counselling process which enables the individual to:

- reflect on currently held skills, interests, knowledge, abilities and achievements;
- think about aspirations;
- gather information on reaching goals;
- determine the feasibility of such goals in the light of personal aptitudes, lifestyle and local and national labour market needs;
- set realistic targets which are understood and realisable, and to which there is personal commitment.

The information collected during one or more IAP sessions leads to the creation of an Individual Action Plan.

Individual Action Plans

An Individual Action Plan is owned by the individual to whom it relates. Nothing should be placed on the Plan with which the individual does not agree. It is produced as a result of an impartial and comprehensive guidance process.

The Plan will include information on the individual's current knowledge, skills and qualifications. It should outline the individual's goals and approximate dates for achieving them. The Plan should record any learning needed to realise the goals. Finally, the Plan should describe the ways to meet any learning needs.

It is essential that everyone involved in devising the Individual Action

Plan appreciate that goals can be altered at any time without incurring any penalties. It is important that the young person remains in charge of their Action Plan. The formulation of goals and their commitment to paper are but aids to the young person. A review date should be included on the Plan.

It is crucial to remember that the individual owns the Plan when decisions are being made about what to include on it and who might have access to it. The individual should be told who may have access to the Plan and the uses to which it might be put.

There are two types of Individual Action Plan: formative documents, which are confidential to the young person; and Plans which are produced at times of transition. These latter Plans are likely to be public, used when negotiating the next stage of education or training or entry into or between sectors of employment.

Why have Individual Action Plans and IAP?

IAP and Individual Action Plans have a number of benefits.

The process of IAP enables adults and young people to gather detailed information about and for the individual young person. Detailed information allows the adult to make effective referrals, offer relevant guidance and ask pertinent questions. Detailed information gives the young person greater understanding of aspirations and learning needs, and encourages informed decision-making.

Through the IAP process young people gain many transferable skills such as time management, personal organisation and decision making. Young people derive satisfaction and confidence through planning and executing an activity. Many gain an awareness of being able to take charge of themselves and their activities.

Why call it 'Individual Action Planning' and an 'Individual Action Plan'?

The central tenet of IAP is that the individual is the primary focus of the Planning process and of the Plan. The centrality of the individual to the process and product means that both are responsive to and reflect individual needs. The process and Plan are intended to assist young people to think more analytically about themselves, their current and future lifestyles and how they might wish to effect changes. IAP shifts control to the individual: this means that IAP cannot be done to another. The individual should determine what happens within their IAP sessions and dictate what appears on their Plans.

Finally, the descriptor 'individual' is used because the IAP session and

Plan can take a holistic view of the young person's personal, social, academic and vocational development. This broad approach will inevitably generate a unique and complex series of learning needs.

Where do Individual Action Plans and IAP lead?

Without a commitment to life-long learning
neither individuals nor countries can develop
or prosper. The learning styles needed to
promote this commitment depend crucially
upon the review and recording of achievement
and upon continuous planning for the future.
National Record of Achievement Guidelines (DES and DFE 1991)

It is clear that IAP processes and Action Plans are not ephemeral things within education, training, guidance and occupational appraisal. Policy-makers, educationalists and employers are increasingly emphasising the importance of life-long learning, personal and occupational development, and of the need for individuals to cultivate flexible approaches towards their employment and education. IAP is a means by which people can be encouraged to take greater responsibility for themselves, and to steer and monitor their own development.

IAP offers immediate benefits to young people and will be central to their later experiences of education and training. It is therefore essential that young people in schools and colleges have the opportunity to experience IAP and to acquire the skills and understanding necessary to ensure that they can engage with these formative assessment processes for their short and longer-term good.

This book has been written to assist those adults teaching and guiding young people to become more effective Individual Action Planners and to derive benefits from this powerful tool of formative assessment.

2 Individual Action Planning

Introduction

This chapter describes the process of IAP. It moves from an overview of the whole IAP cycle to a review of each stage within the process, describing the skills necessary for undertaking IAP.

What is Individual Action Planning?

IAP is a formative and cyclic process placing the young person at its centre. It enables the learner to:

- become aware of and acknowledge achievements, interests, competences and prior learning;
- explore personal, educational and vocational aspirations
- consider alternative goals and aspirations;
- have access to unbiased and plentiful information, which should be accompanied by impartial counselling;
- make informed decisions about future goals and set achievable short-, medium and long-term targets to help realise these goals;
- review progress towards specified targets and goals at appropriate intervals, in order to modify or change their plans as necessary.

IAP expands young people's awareness and their sense of personal potential. It does not close down an individual's options or force early vocational decisions. From the outset of the IAP process, it should be made clear to the young person and the adult planning partner that ideas canvassed during IAP sessions and any ensuing targets are not necessarily, nor punitively, binding. Essential to IAP is the emphasis placed on exploration, discussion and tentativeness. Equally important are its ongoing nature and the review sessions which allow systematic consideration of progress and of the appropriateness of the Action Plan.

There are, in theory, no limits to the number of times which an individual may go through the IAP process. Limitations are determined by such pragmatic constraints such as the availability of time, other demands on the young person and access to an adult planning partner.

In its most basic form the IAP cycle can be illustrated as in Figure 2.1. If the IAP cycle is to be effective, it is important that young people and planning partners understand its contributory elements.

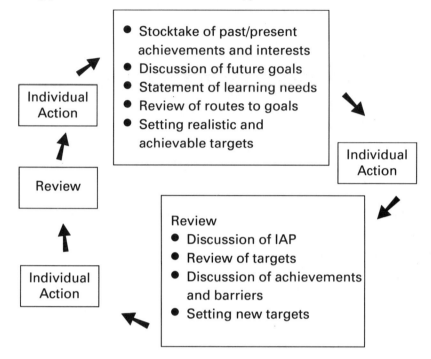

Figure 2.1

The Essential Elements of IAP

The IAP cycle involves the young person in:

1 Raising self-awareness.
2 Considering broad aspirations.
3 Identifying development needs.
4 Collecting relevant information and discussing with an impartial counsellor aspirations, learning needs and education or training options.
5 Planning broad goals.
6 Setting smaller actionable targets which are time-bound and accompanied by success criteria to facilitate monitoring.
7 Reviewing actions and experiences and re-formulating targets, timescales or even broad goals if necessary.

1 Raising Self-Awareness

In order to be effective, young people need self-knowledge. They need to be made aware of their current skills, achievements and interests, and of the ways in which they like to learn most effectively. They need some concept of their vocational or educational aspirations and their envisioned lifestyle. In the immediate term, young people need a sense of themselves and how they might choose to develop.

Without self-knowledge, young people may underestimate their own achievements and set themselves insufficiently challenging targets. They may devise targets which reflect dated or inappropriate goals, or they try to undertake learning in ways which, for them, are likely to be doomed to failure. The more self-aware young people are and the more aware they are of what is available and happening around them, the more likely it is that the IAP session will be successful.

Young people do have access to a range of sources of information about themselves. These sources will vary according to the age of the young person and the type of educational provision they are offered. Young people will need to be aware of the various possibilities for collecting and making use of such sources. Information may be collected in Personal and Social Education sessions (PSE), during work experience and through careers education.

Young people will be able to build up a profile of their learning through the formative assessment work undertaken in specific curricular areas. Such information can be synthesised during discussions with teachers or tutors in preparation for completing Records of Achievement. Teaching staff should be able to help young people analyse what staff say about their learning and to analyse their own responses to various learning situations.

Beyond the institution young people will have access to much information about themselves through extra-mural activities, from organisations or groups to which they belong, through part-time employment, and from their peers and family. Young people need to be taught how to identify, collect and make use of such information.

Adult planning partners will need to help young people explore their self-image, and consider with them their qualities and competences. Often young people and adults are not familiar with thinking about qualities and competences. They may, for example, fail to stand back from an activity or task to determine what general skills or competences have been demonstrated. Young people and teachers are likely to welcome assistance in this.

In helping young people develop self-awareness, teaching staff may also need to be reminded that it is possible to sustain a jaundiced opinion of certain young people and that such preconceptions have to be put to one side or the IAP dialogue will be less open and effective. Finally, teachers need to be reminded of the dangers of importing their own values into the IAP session and of the risks of discounting or devaluing what young people may consider their achievements or skills.

There are many activities which can be used to encourage young people to take stock of themselves, some examples of which follow in the next chapter.

2 Considering Goals or Aspirations

There are two main and diametrically opposed ways to approach IAP and thus individual development.

The first involves the young person and planning partner in determining what the young person has not achieved and in which areas he or she may be weakest. From this review flow targets which constitute remedial action. Although this may occasionally be a useful approach and one which young people often light upon, it is not the best model for good action planning. If consistently employed it will create a sense of deficiency. Young people will experience themselves as continually falling short and any sense of self-esteem generated through consideration of past achievements and experiences could be undermined.

In approaching IAP from the stance of remedying weaknesses there are further inherent dangers in that the targets which are set may be ones which reflect standards and values which are not those of the young person, but which match parent, tutor, school, or college needs. Where young people feel compelled to accept such targets, they are not likely to feel overly motivated to achieve them and the IAP process may be seen to be another bureaucratic exercise which compounds a sense of failure. The dangers of IAP being misappropriated by the institution are addressed in Chapter 6.

The second approach to IAP is to consider it as a vehicle to assist the realisation of self-generated goals. Thus, the young person considers broadly what he or she might like to do or to become. These broad goals can be discussed with the planning partner to determine feasibility and desirability, and to explore the implications of setting out to realise such goals. This style of planning is likely to be more effective as the goals are self-generated and will reflect individuals' needs.

Having determined the broad aim and a starting point, the learner and planning partner can begin to define the young person's learning and information needs, shape and refine the goal and finally, decide on the smaller steps towards realising the goal.

3 and 4 Identifying learning and information needs

Once the young person has decided upon a broad goal, and what realising it might entail, a systematic process of information gathering ensues. The young person may need to acquire information or new skills, or develop existing ones. Determining learning and information needs is best done in conjunction with the planning partner. The complexion of this stage of the planning cycle will vary according to the individual, the aspiration and perhaps the age of the individual. It may, for example, be a more pro-tracted process at a time of transition when the young person is collecting and assessing information about training and educational courses and particular occupational areas, and trying to establish the most appropriate point of entry. The young person may be working with the planning part-ner to identify relevant sources of information and undergoing a process of referral to various occupational, training or educational advisers. Younger students or those not at points of transition may have less com-plex decisions to make. They may need less information and no referrals. This phase may, therefore, be much briefer.

There may, however, be occasions when although young people are not making decisions about their future careers or education, issues arise which will require more lengthy IAP counselling. Such issues as settling into a new school or college, dealing with learning problems, or trying to consider aspects of personal development or personal relationships will require time, to allow the young person to examine the issues and pro-pose courses of action.

Once young people have acquired the necessary information, they can think further about their broad goals or aspirations. Some may be able to refine their long-term aims, and work out specific steps towards their goals. Others may decide to change course in the light of information they have found or to abandon their original goal. The opportunity for young people to change their minds within a structured situation is important. IAP sessions should allow young people to collect and analyse information and to reject a goal, and to experience this as a legit-imate part of the decision-making process. IAP has an educative role in helping people develop effective decision-making skills.

5 Broad Planning

While still at the stage of broad planning, young people should be encouraged to consider alternative routes to realising their goals. Map-ping alternative routes at an early stage allows the young person to select the one to which he or she feels greatest commitment, but it also creates a sense of security for the individual in knowing that there are other routes to achieving goals. This encourages an awareness that one course of action need not be doggedly pursued, but can be exchanged for another viable one. This type of forward planning is particularly important when a goal is predicted upon unpredictable factors, such as exam results, the availability of funding, or acceptance onto a course.

Just as planning may be unfamiliar to students, so may sketching out alternative courses of action. Until students understand that this is useful, it may arouse students' criticism.

6 Setting Actionable Targets

This is one of the hardest aspects of the IAP process, both conceptually and in practice. It is hard, because people are often unused to thinking about breaking down a broad aim into a series of small steps. It demands a real clarity of goal and a clear understanding of how it can be achieved, and how progress might be measured.

Like the overall process of broad planning and informed decision-making, creating actionable steps may be perceived as delaying the gratification derived from achievement. It does, however, ensure that individuals launch themselves on a course of action knowing what they have to do and being able to monitor what they have completed. The following prompts may help teaching staff and young people as they embark upon the target setting process:

1. Think about all the things which need to be done.
2. Decide upon the best order in which to do things.
3. Decide how best to make use of resources (e.g. time, money, other people and materials).
4. Determine what the implications of your plans might be.
5. Try to work our what problems might occur and how they might be confronted.
6. Now write out what has to be done as small tasks. Decide on the task, what it should lead to, who might help and how, and the date by which you want it completed.

7 Reviewing

The final element of the planning cycle is that of reviewing. Success at this stage is dependent upon the extent to which targets or action steps have previously been clearly defined. Targets need to be evaluated against their expected outcomes, the date by which tasks should have been completed and the ways in which the tasks contribute sequentially to the realisation of the longer-term aim. The rationale behind reviewing should be explained to students. It should be made clear that IAP review sessions are part of the formative and forward-looking planning process. Reviewing is an opportunity to reconsider goals and routes, to think about what may have facilitated or impeded progress, and to determine what has been gained through pursuing targets.

The review cycle requires from the planning partner and learner the skills of listening, questioning, exploring and trying to substantiate statements. The air of a review session should be conducive to honest appraisal, to praise and encouragement, and to discussing doubts and concerns. Throughout the review session it should be made clear that success or failure is not an absolute, that there are gradations of both, and that both are opportunities for learning and starting points for future actions, and that personal standards are important. Learners, overly dependent upon being marked and trapped into believing that teaching staff function solely to determine 'pass' or 'fail' may find the review process quite alien.

Each stage of IAP needs to be explored with students, so they understand its rationale and possible outcomes and the ways in which each stage contributes to the next. Young people should also be aware of their own and others' roles at each stage. Comprehensive explanation and answering students' questions will allow them to understand and to engage more thoughtfully with IAP processes.

How Can IAP Be Undertaken Most Effectively?

IAP throws teaching staff and students into new roles, ones with which they may initially feel uncomfortable and which will demand new skills. For IAP to be most effective, teaching staff and students need to know:

- why they are doing IAP;
- what IAP involves;
- the implications of IAP;
- what IAP requires of them;
- what they may expect of each other;
- what support, training or additional information might be available;
- how IAP will be undertaken.

Enhancing Understanding of IAP

Thus far the chapter has described the various stages in the cycle and the ways in which each leads to the next. Staff and young people need an understanding of the IAP cycle, in order to feel engaged and not the passive recipients of an imposed and fragmentary series of activities.

Empowering people by sharing with them the whole is but part of effectively explaining IAP. The second stage in developing staff and students' understanding is a rehearsal of the potential benefits of IAP. Without sharing this information, there is little reason why either staff or students should be prepared to undertake IAP, nor any reason why they should feel commitment to the process.

The Benefits To Young People Of Individual Action Planning

Evaluations of a range of IAP projects and practices in schools, colleges and youth training have revealed a number of benefits. (see Squirrell, 1991, 1992a; Watts, 1992). Through IAP young people may derive:

- increased self-awareness, self-confidence and self-esteem;
- a sense of what they have achieved, and what they may achieve in the future;
- some legitimation of their aspirations;
- the opportunity to set themselves challenges;
- a sense of security from the planning relationship and from talking through their ideas and plans;
- a sense of security through the focused collection and discussion of information relevant to their futures;
- increased motivation;
- satisfaction from making better use of their time and taking increased responsibility for themselves.

Through developing IAP skills, young people acquire a range of personal competences, such as time-management, planning and monitoring skills, and an awareness of their use of resources. Young people can become adept problem-solvers and gain a number of information-handling skills. Through working with others, often adults who are strangers to them, young people gain skills in self-presentation, self-advocacy and negotiation.

Developing skills and increasing self-awareness can help young people deal more effectively with the daily demands of their education and training courses, and help them plan, complete and present assignments. Such skills can also assist the productive use of leisure time.

IAP assists decision-making, a sense of self-determination and feelings of control. Through IAP young people may be more likely to experience coherence in their education and training, and greater progression as they live through various phases of their personal and public lives.

Benefits to Teaching and Tutoring Staff

Individual Action Planning offer teachers and tutors a series of opportunities for developing detailed knowledge of young people's achievements, prior learning experiences, competences and interests. In the long term this enables them to offer thorough and responsive counselling, relevant information and to make the most effective referrals. This can only improve professional relationships with young people and lead to an increased sense of professional satisfaction for staff.

IAP sessions can offer teachers and tutors:

- a clearer tutoring role;
- an enhanced rapport with young people;
- an enhancement to RoA process and the final RoA document;
- a way to deliver individual learning aspects within the National Curriculum;
- a mechanism to manage flexible learning;
- young people who are able to identify their learning needs and who become motivated problem-solvers.

IAP involving information collection and referrals encourages staff to communicate with colleagues within and beyond a single institution. It encourages greater understanding of other people's subject areas and roles.

Benefits of IAP to Careers Officers

Careers Officers gain when young people have been engaged in Action Planning processes. Young people may come to them with more extensive documentation about themselves. They arrive with greater self-awareness and many will have a more focused understanding of their career options and training needs. Having engaged in negotiation during the Action Planning process means that many young people will be more able to ask for what they want. Careers Guidance sessions can often be more detailed and wide ranging, and more flexible and responsive to young people's actual needs.

Benefits for Young People's Future Employers and Trainers

Young people who have experienced IAP process are likely to be more effective at interview, more able to talk coherently about themselves and to ask with some authority for what they want and need to do next. Through choosing their training and employment routes more carefully, they may settle more speedily into their working roles. Young people with greater self-awareness may be more effective in dealing with the move into adult life. Through IAP young people may have greater insights into work-place appraisal processes and be more adept when discussing their own occupational development.

Training

Young people will need to develop self-awareness and skills of critical reflection. They will need to think about their aims and aspirations and discuss these in the context of what they know of themselves, their preferred learning styles, interests and current achievement levels. Young people will need to be trained in target setting and in monitoring their progress, and to become skilled in perceiving and creating opportunities for realising their learning goals and targets.

Young people need to be able to accept and deal with their own centrality in the process and in the execution of their plans. They may need training to take responsibility for themselves and not to rely on teaching staff.

Likewise teaching staff will need to be trained and to reconsider their view of young people. They will need to discourage students' dependency and encourage independent decision-making and responsibility for action. They will need to accept young people's assessment of progress, discuss evidence and assist in the evaluation of achievements.

Chapter 3 offers some exercises which may help teaching staff to foster IAP skills in young people. Tutoring staff may also need training, particularly in developing and refining skills in questioning and listening. They need to develop the skills to create an atmosphere in which young people feel they can openly explore aspects of themselves, and consider their futures, ambitions and aspirations. The exploratory and sometimes tentative nature of IAP sessions requires great sensitivity from those adults working with young people.

Ideally IAP should take the form of discussion, when questions may be used to stimulate the young person to think about her or himself. However, questioning should be limited so that the time which is available can be maximally used by the young person to talk about aspects of him or herself, table concerns and reach some decisions about immediate, if not longer-term, actions. Adults can facilitate this by using many of the skills of good counselling. Such skills include:

- offering the young person full and non-judgemental attention;
- listening carefully and not importing meaning, nor trying to hear what is most expected, nor what the teacher thinks most desirable;
- offering serious acceptance of what the young person says, but

being prepared to help identify contradictions and areas of confusion;

- prompting the young person to explore or explain further through open-ended questions or comments;
- feeding back to the young person what has been said, to ensure common understanding and that there has been no misinterpretation on the adult's part, and to help the young person consolidate his or her thinking;
- not censoring nor overlooking what is of significance to the young person.

Questioning and listening are explored further in Chapter 7. Staff may also need some training in helping young people plan future action. Teaching staff need to be counselled to allow the young person to move at his or her own pace. Thus, they need to be alerted to the dangers of offering advice, giving clear objectives or directions, or trying to impose actions or targets which may seem desirable to them. Staff may need to be counselled to refrain from trying to dismiss something as not feasible rather than allowing the young person to discover that for him/herself. Teaching staff need to be warned of the dangers of allowing young people to be dependent upon adults or other authority figures and, where young people lack their own ideas, trying to draw directions and instructions from an adult.

Teaching staff will need to be equipped to deal with situations where the young person faces challenges to realising his or her goals. The teacher will have to assist a young person to appreciate the existence and effects of such constraints, to realising a goal. Constraints may be particular to the young person, for example, poor educational achievement, a young person's lifestyle preferences or a particular physical feature such as colour blindness. Where possible, barriers should be exposed and ways found to circumnavigate them. Other constraints might be external, for example local and national labour market needs, the cost, accessibility or type of further education and training. Such issues need to be explored and possible solutions sought. It may be that in trying to confront constraints the help and advice of other agencies becomes necessary.

In any training programme, teaching staff will need to discuss target setting and the roles they may play in this phase of IAP. There are a few clear rules which should be observed when helping to create targets. Targets should be achievable, understood and the young person has to feel commitment to them. Targets should consist of a number of small steps which are time-bound. The young person should be helped to set him or herself success criteria so that it is clear when targets have been met. Likely sources of help should also be identified. The most common problems with target setting lie in the young person not understanding or not having any real commitment to the target. Broad aims or statements such as: 'pass my GCSEs well', 'get better in French', 'learn how to drive' and 'get on better with my parents' are not targets and cannot be allowed to pass as such.

Part of the process of informing and training students and staff will be to ensure that both are aware of their own and the other's role. Thus far it has been emphasised that IAP demands that the traditional roles of teacher and student are re-considered, so that the young person is empowered, is central and feels in control of the process. The young person has to become pro-active and be able to explore ideas and thoughts.

It is important that young people are equipped to deal with the centrality of their role as this differs from many other of their educational and training activities. Young people need to feel comfortable in this role. In encouraging the young person to feel in control the parameters for the session should be discussed – for example, its length – what ground might be covered, and how sensitive or confidential issues might be handled. This discussion protects adult and the young person.

Confidentiality will in part be dictated by school or college policies on certain issues and the teacher's own sense of accountability and professional responsibility in others. It is, however, useful if the young person knows what, if anything, others may be told. It is clear that teachers need to know their institution's policies before embarking upon IAP.

The session should not leave the young person feeling unduly probed nor intruded upon. Adults need to be aware that some young people are unused to or dislike talking about themselves. The young person should not feel mocked or judged, or devalued in their own or someone else's eyes, and should not feel railroaded into talking or signing up to unwanted goals.

The young person should leave the IAP sessions feeling:

- listened to;
- in control of what has taken place;
- positive about him or herself;
- positive about achievements and interests;
- motivated to work towards targets;
- aware of any possible sources of help;
- that he or she fully understands what has taken place and why;
- fully aware of the next stages within the IAP process.

This overview of the IAP process has addressed the various stages within the IAP cycle. It has discussed the possible outcomes and some of the more problematic aspects of each of these stages.

In answering the question how can IAP be most effectively done, the chapter has made three recommendations. These are that students and staff be empowered to participate and manage the process for themselves. Thus they need to be fully aware of what is involved in each stage of the whole cycle, and the various outcomes and pitfalls. Secondly, to be able to act on the knowledge of IAP and to feel comfortable and in control of the processes both staff and students will require training.

Finally, they need to know what the possible benefits of IAP might be. Such knowledge will act as a motivator and will be useful as an aid to checking on the outcomes of the whole process.

3 Raising Awareness and Skilling Young People

Introduction

This chapter offers a number of activities which are intended to help young people develop and practise skills which will enable them more effectively to manage their role in the IAP process.

The exemplar material in this chapter is intended to stimulate practitioners' thinking. Not all suggestions will meet the needs of all learners. The range of material should, however, demonstrate that it is possible to cultivate IAP skills with people of all ages and levels of current achievements.

Many of the exercises and suggestions could be incorporated into the tutorial or personal and social education programmes which colleges and schools already undertake. However, not all practitioners will be in a position to integrate IAP skills into tutorial programmes. Limitations on time and resources have to be recognised. It is hoped that some of the exercises suggested in this chapter can still be used where preparation time for IAP is very limited. It is clear from evaluations of IAP that young people benefit from thinking about themselves and their future goals before embarking upon IAP.

There is no ideal age at which to start doing IAP with young people. Evaluation work shows practitioners and young people themselves suggesting that the earlier IAP begins, the better. This has led to beginning IAP with pupils in years 6 and 7. It is clear from evaluation that the longer young people have to experience the process-based elements of IAP, the more effective they will be at creating Individual Action Plans at later transition stages.

There are long-term gains from cultivating such skills as enhancing self-understanding, awareness of time and its use, decision-making and the ability to check on the progress of plans. The more young people can practise such skills and see how they relate to one another, the more likely that they will become habits for managing daily life.

The following pages offer suggestions for ways to cultivate the skills which underpin the four stages of effective IAP: taking stock and raising awareness; thinking about time and planning how best to use it; setting actionable targets, and reviewing progress towards set goals.

Section 1: Raising Self-Awareness

The following material is intended to help young people to think about themselves and to appreciate what is to be gained from having self-knowledge. In working with young people to heighten their self-awareness, the teacher, tutor or guidance worker is expected to act only as a facilitator. He or she should not try to conduct a full-scale personality audit nor engage in amateur psychoanalysis. The adult will need to pay attention to group dynamics, to what is possible within a group, and to observe the ways in which individuals respond to self-awareness-raising activities. Some young people find thinking about themselves not only an alien activity but an uncomfortable and threatening one.

Young people have to be encouraged to explore their strengths as well as their weaknesses. Some young people dwell at interminable length on their weaknesses, ignoring their many competences, qualities and areas of prowess. Engaging with students' limited sense of self-esteem will be tricky, but unless they are encouraged to encounter and question their skewed sense of self from the outset, their evaluation of their own progress in the light of their Action Plans and targets is likely to be equally warped. These young people have to realise that self-awareness is about the recognition and appreciation of strengths as well as weaknesses. They have to be taught that there is no virtue in false modesty and no stigma or boastfulness in finding and acknowledging personal strengths.

At the other extreme, some young people have no recognition of their weaknesses and a limited awareness of the extent to which they really are competent. In working with this group of young people the adult will need to try to tease out an awareness of areas which may be cultivated and develop a critical questioning of areas in which young people may delude themselves about the effectiveness of their skills.

In fostering self-questioning the tutor must veer away from any temptation to interfere in the way in which young people construct themselves, or to tell them how they ought to be. In thinking about themselves, young people will be questioning their own value systems, thinking about what is of importance to them and about the ways in which they want to impact on their environment and on other people. When discussing personal values adults should be careful not to criticise.

Tutors who are trying to teach self-awareness in young people will need to know why they are doing this. Some young people will find the process uncomfortable or will be fearful that they will simply see themselves as a disturbing bundle of weaknesses and deficits. Others may be glib about the process. Some may be reluctant to give time to an activity which does not obviously yield a tangible result. Some may try to claim that they are 'too old to change'. Tutors need to handle such young people's comments, concerns and criticisms with sensitivity.

Teachers will need to think carefully about how they will structure a programme of awareness-raising activities and ensure that they are appropriate and challenging, yet do not arouse antagonism. The teacher will need to tell young people why they are undertaking activities which may prove to be difficult. The tutor may rehearse some of the reasons for increasing self-awareness with young people and may offer some of the following. Self-knowledge can help young people to:

- deal with periods of personal stress by allowing them to think beforehand about the ways in which they may react and deal most effectively with problems;
- meet periods of change and transition with an awareness of personal coping strategies;
- be aware that they can effect changes to their lives and within themselves;
- be more in control of themselves and of their ways of behaving;
- be confident that they are behaving appropriately and are able to address problems in their relationships with family, friends and others;
- present themselves more effectively, for example at a job or college interview;
- be able to write about themselves more clearly and extensively when, for example, they complete a Record of Achievement, a personal statement or an application form;
- be more 'in tune' with themselves, having a clearer picture of themselves and being more realistic about themselves and what they undertake;
- make more realistic decisions about their futures.

The following exercises are intended to help young people think about themselves.

1 Life Lines

Students are asked to consider their lives to date in graphic form in order to encourage them to consider any particular patterns or traits.

Students should be asked to draw a line or snake shape which represents their life to date. Along the line they should plot significant events, successes, disappointments and the turning points in their lives. Students should be asked to reflect on all aspects of their lives. They will need time to re-visit their life-line, as plotting one event is likely to spark recollection of another.

Having drawn their life-line students can be asked to consider and record their responses to the following.

Students should consider:

- why they choose a particular shape to illustrate their life-line;
- whether they can detect any patterns or themes in their lives;
- whether they made choices or drifted into changes of direction;
- what contributed to high or low points in their lives;
- what can be learnt from reflecting on the high or low points of their lives and on any emerging patterns.

2 Who Am I?

Students are asked to write in list form their qualities and strengths. These lists become the basis for future action.

1. Young people should be asked to make a list of their strengths. They should evidence their statements.
2. Students should make a second list of aspects about themselves which they would like to improve and to note why they wish to do so.
3. A third list should be made of things which although not strengths are not things they want to change about themselves. Students should be asked to note why they do not want to change some aspects of themselves.

This data can be used in several ways. Some may like to talk about their lists with another. This sharing takes trust, listening skills and the ability to stand firm if another disagrees. However, the sharing process has many advantages, it may, for example, reveal a lack of self-knowledge or a tendency towards underestimation.

Others may like to take their lists a stage further and think about the aspects of themselves they may want to develop. Alongside actively thinking about strategies for so doing, young people can work with peers, family, friends or others. Certainly where more specific aspects for self-development are identified, the young person might like to approach a teacher, employer or guidance worker who may have particular observations or suggestions.

3 Things I know about Myself

Some young people might feel easier thinking about themselves within a more structured form. There are a number of ways in which this can be done. Some examples of proformas which young people can complete follow below are in Tables 3.1–3.4. Some require a simple box ticking and others brief comments. It is important that such lists are not solely focused on academic or training-based attainments.

Table 3.1 What am I like?

WHAT AM I LIKE: (Tick the box which applies to you)	Almost always	Usually	Not often	Rarely
Cheerful				
Aggressive				
Moody				
Affectionate				
Emotional				
Caring				
Ambitious				
Determined				
Self-critical				
Imaginative				
Conscientious				
Trustworthy				
Honest				
Responsible				
Persevering				

Table 3.2 What am I like with other people?

WHAT AM I LIKE WITH OTHER PEOPLE (Tick the box which applies to you)	Almost always	Usually	Not often	Rarely
Good mixer				
Get on well with own age group				
Get on well with adults				
Speak easily and well				
Have a number of friends				
Friendly by nature				
Get on well with parents				
Get on well with teachers				
Able to work well with others				
Able to listen to other people's ideas				
Like helping others				
Like being on my own				
Able to put forward my own ideas even if they're different from other people's				

Table 3.3 What am I like about work and my attitude to it?

WHAT AM I LIKE ABOUT WORK AND MY ATTIUDE TO IT (Tick the box which applies to you)	It's me	It's not me	I'd like it to be me	Not interested
I can work hard				
I do persevere				
I'm keen to succeed				
I'm good at sports				
I can work quickly				
I complete my homework				
I can concentrate				
I can work out revision timetables				
I can revise for exams				
I do meet coursework deadlines				
I can solve problems				
I can work on my own				
I can work with a group of people				
I can put forward my own ideas				
I listen to other people's ideas				
I make up my own mind				
I do ask questions in class				
I do answer questions in class				
I am good at academic subjects generally				
I am good at practical subjects generally				

Table 3.4 (Oldham YDP)

Activities out of school

Are you or have you been a member of any of the following clubs or organisations?

guides/scouts ☐ girls'/boys' brigade ☐ youth club ☐ mosque/chapel/church ☐

sports team(s) ☐ band/choir ☐ dance group or class ☐ drama group or class ☐

angling ☐ photography ☐ voluntary work group ☐ night/evening class ☐

Have we missed anything? ☐

Are you interested in or have had a go at any of the following?

photography ☐ angling ☐ cycling ☐ walking/hiking ☐ camping ☐

sailing ☐ cars/motor bikes ☐ judo/karate/martial arts ☐ dress making ☐

stamp/coin collecting ☐ dancing ☐ drama ☐ keep fit ☐ computing ☐

cookery ☐ pets ☐ football ☐ cricket ☐ painting/drawing ☐ making things ☐

TV ☐ reading ☐ pen friends ☐ newspapers ☐ current affairs ☐

hospital visiting ☐ baby sitting ☐

Have we missed anything? ☐

Look again at these last three sections, choose three things you have done, or are doing, and say what you feel you have gained from then and what skills you now have.

The dangers in only making use of lists arises if they encourage young people to be reactive and to limit their thinking to simple box-ticking. This can be counteracted by the ways in which the lists are used once completed.

Younger pupils may also want some structures for thinking about themselves, but find tables and lists intimidating. Figures 3.1 and 3.2 show two suggestions for younger pupils.

Figure 3.1 The different pieces of my life

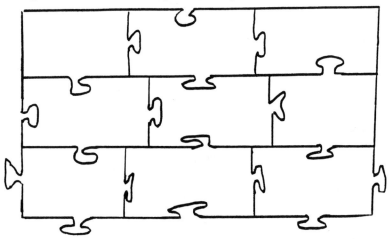

Complete the jig saw pieces by writing about different aspects of yourself. You may like to write about:

- your hobbies
- your thoughts about school
- your family
- your friends
- where you live
- the things you like doing
- the types of things you dislike the most
- your fantasies

Young people with special needs can construct similar sets of statements about themselves without having to make use of check-lists, pens and paper. Access to IT equipment, symbol banks and the skills to make use of a mouse means that 'dragging' symbols which appear on a screen can create profiles of themselves. The symbols may be created by scanning or pictures, or through the purchase of commercial packages such as the Rebus symbols (Figure 3.3).

Figure 3.2 Think about the sort of person you are. The words on the page may help you. Put any words which apply to you in the circle and add as many others as you like.

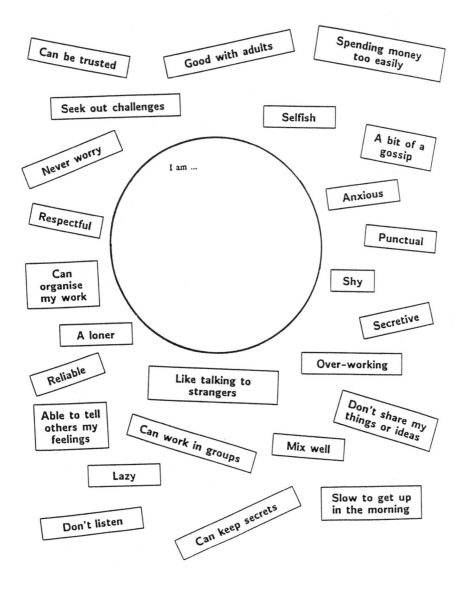

Figure 3.3 Examples of Rebus symbols (Supplied by St. Francis School, Lincoln.)

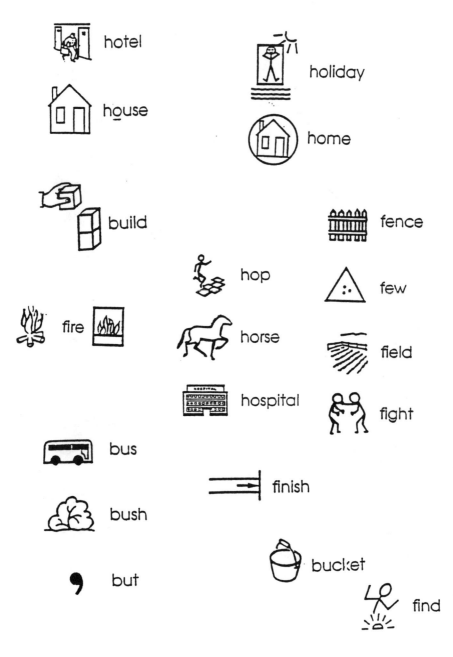

Symbol, word-based or tick-box lists which generate ideas and statements can be used as the basis of discussion with a fellow pupil, teacher, tutor or other adult carer. Young people may like to consider the accuracy of their self-image, how it compares with those held by others, and what aspects of themselves they have failed to consider or chosen to present and what this may also reveal about themselves. For those who prefer to undertake oral brain-storming, an activity follows below.

4 Who am I? Brain-Storming in Pairs

1. Young people can be asked to work in pairs, each telling the other 10 things about him or herself, for example:

I am bossy;
I think that other people like to have me as a friend;
I prefer to work on my own rather than in a group.

2. The pairs can discuss the statements, comparing each other's view.
3. During this stage the young people should find evidence for their statements. They should reflect upon the balance of good and bad they thought about for themselves and the other and what significance this has, if any.

The natural extension to thinking about oneself is to consider how one might wish to change. At this stage brain-storming activities can be tried. Figure 3.4 may help some students to think about themselves in the future.

Figure 3.4 Think about who you are now and put words in the top circle. Then think about the sort of person you would like to be and put those words in the bottom circle

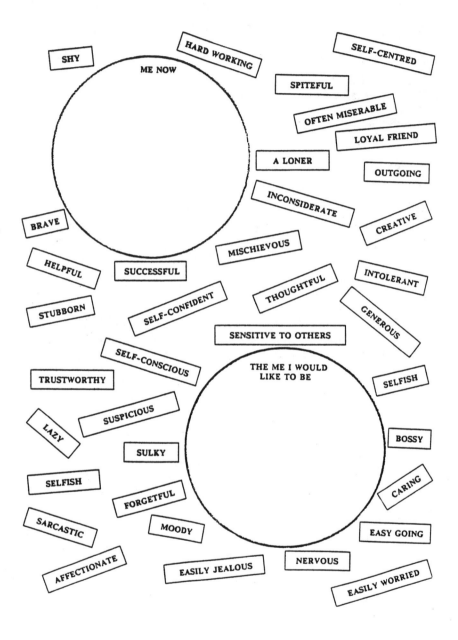

Students' Use Of Time

Part of developing a personal profile is to reflect on how an individual values and uses resources such as time. The following exercises ask students to consider their use of time. This will offer useful insights for the young person into him or herself. Additionally, young people may be encouraged to think about future use of time.

5 *Reviewing the week*

Give students copies of the grids. As their week progresses, ask them to fill in how much time they are spending (Table 3.5):

- sleeping;
- eating;
- watching TV;
- socialising with friends;
- doing school or college work;
- pursuing other activities – ask them to specify.

Students can devise their own colour code or symbol systems for completing their grids.

Table 3.5 (From *Developing Personal Effectiveness*, COIC.)

	morning					afternoon						
	12-2	2-4	4-6	6-8	8-10	10-12	12–2	2–4	4-6	6-8	8-10	10-12
Mon												
Tues												
Wed												
Thur												
Fri												
Sat												
Sun												

At the end of the week ask students to analyse their grids. They should note how much time they spend overall on:

- sleeping;
- being at school or college;
- socialising etc.

If students so wish these aggregated totals can be represented in a pie-chart.

Students should be asked to reflect honestly on

- where in the week and over what tasks they may be wasting time;
- what surprises them about their use of time;
- whether and where they spend time doing things which they don't want to do;
- how much of their time they really enjoy.

Students can be encouraged to ask themselves global questions about their use of time, such as:

- am I happy about the ways I use my time?
- do I make decisions about how I spend my time?
- why do I do things I don't want to do? What can I do about this?
- do I make excuses such as: 'I haven't got the time', 'there's not enough time', 'there's nothing to do where I live' or 'I can't think of anything else to do'?
- could I organise my time more effectively?
- what else could I do with my time if I could organise it more effectively?

Using Leisure Time

6 Leisure Questionnaires

Young people may need some help in thinking about how they spend their time and in generating ideas for how they might use their leisure time. Tables 3.6 and 3.7 show several grids which young people may work through, and which offer ideas on using time.

Table 3.6 Leisure Time. Here is a list of things that you might do in your spare time. Tick any activity which you do, add any others in the spaces provided, and circle the five things which you enjoy the most.

Watching television		Playing an instrument		Listen to the radio	
Going to discos		Listening to records		Reading	
Going to Youth Club		Golf		Dancing	
Swimming		Guides/scouts		St John's/Red Cross	
Squash		Tennis		Netball	
Canoeing		Basketball		Cricket	
Horse riding		Soccer		Cooking	
Outdoor pursuits		Drawing/painting		Fishing	
Computers		Drama		Writing to pen friends	
Badminton		Sewing		Camping	
Athletics		Gymnastics		Cinema	
Shopping		Goint out to eat		Rugby	
Stamp collecting		Skateboarding		Volleyball	
Hockey		Ice skating		Boxing	
Martial arts		Aerobics		Weight training	
Ten-pin bowling		Jogging		Hockey	
Model making		Cycling		Fell walking	
Train spotting		Writing stories		Snooker	
Darts		Watching sport		Rock climbing	
Keeping pets		Gardening		Bird watching	
Part-time job					

Table 3.7 'Leisure Time' Worksheet. How do you spend your time? Place a √ in the appropriate box. (From Hopson and Scully, *Lifeskills*.)

Activity	Daily	Weekly	Monthly	Rarely	Never
Sleeping (other than at night)					
Going for a walk					
Participating in organised games/sport					
Watching sport					
Jogging					
Climbing					
Canoeing					
Gardening					
Going to the theatre					
Attending concerts					
Riding					
Walking a dog(s)					
Decorating					
Listening to records/tapes					
Watching TV					
Part-time Job					
Doing nothing					
Going to the cinema					
Disco dancing					
Ice-skating					
Visiting friends					
Doing house-work					
Voluntary work					
Youth club					
Listening to the radio					
Attending organisations such as Scouts, Guides, St. Johns etc.					
Attending church					
Cycling					
Roller skating					

7 Brain-storming about Leisure Time

The purpose of this exercise is to encourage students to think about the range of things which they might do.

In groups, young people work through a bundle of local newspapers to list what leisure activities and options are available in the area. Information can be found in the small ads and the articles as well as the leisure and events pages. Having created lists – such as horse-riding, cinema, theatre, ice-skating, local rambles, jumble sales, fashion shows, coin collecting, flying lessons – young people should each choose one activity and find out more about it. They could collect information under such headings as:

- location and travel arrangements to the activity;
- its cost;
- whether special equipment is needed;
- whether tuition is needed;
- how to book or participate;
- whether it is seasonal;
- whether it is undertaken alone or in groups.

At this stage it will be possible to create a leisure information file. Young people should be encouraged to undertake to try out a new activity and report back to the group.

Section 2: Planning the use of Time

Having thought about how time is spent and how it might be little used, young people are ready to move onto planning their time. There are a number of ways in which this might be done, for example through use of diaries, Funfaxes, school students' Filofaxes, and school- or college-devised year planners. Tables 3.8–3.9 show a range of planning aids.

Table 3.8

Residential Experience Diary	Residential Experience Diary
First Day	**Second Day**
What are the AIMS of the Course? _____	What did you do today and what activity did you enjoy the most? __
What are YOUR targets for the week? _____	Have there been any safety precautions that you have had to take?
What are your first impressions of the Centre (or the first night's stop) and its surroundings? _____	Describe three things that you have found out about yourself today?
How do you feel now the Course has started? _____	

Table 3.9(a) Term planner (Produced by St. Guthlac School, Lincolnshire.)

	Subjects	Homework
Monday		
Tuesday		
Wednes-day		
Thursday		
Friday		

Table 3.9(a) (Continued) Term planner (Produced by St. Guthlac School, Lincolnshire.)

	Date			Date			Date			Date	
Mon			Mon			Mon			Mon		
Tues			Tues			Tues			Tues		
Wed			Wed			Wed			Wed		
Thurs			Thurs			Thurs			Thurs		
Fri			Fri			Fri			Fri		
Mon			Mon			Mon			Mon		
Tues			Tues			Tues			Tues		
Wed			Wed			Wed			Wed		
Thurs			Thurs			Thurs			Thurs		
Fri			Fri			Fri			Fri		
Mon			Mon			Mon			Mon		
Tues			Tues			Tues			Tues		
Wed			Wed			Wed			Wed		
Thurs			Thurs			Thurs			Thurs		
Fri			Fri			Fri			Fri		
Mon			Mon			Mon			Mon		
Tues			Tues			Tues			Tues		
Wed			Wed			Wed			Wed		
Thurs			Thurs			Thurs			Thurs		
Fri			Fri			Fri			Fri		

Table 3.9(b) Produced by Cambridgeshire Careers Service for its Y.D.P.

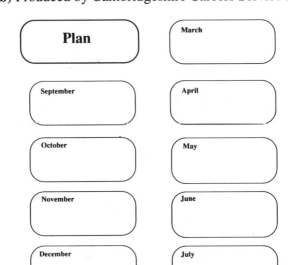

Plan	March
September	April
October	May
November	June
December	July
January	August
February	September

Table 3.9(c) Positive achievements this term (sport, school activities, special events) (Cambridgeshire Careers Service.)

Targets achieved during the year

| | Student Signature | Tutor Signature |

Table 3.10 Key events. Tick which of these events will affect you during the next year (Sept–Sept) and when

Tick	Event	When (date or roughly when)
	1. Your birthday	
	2. School holidays/term dates	
	3. Final Record of Achievement interview	
	4. Careers Convention	
	5. Field trip/s	
	6. Take RoA profile home	
	7. Mock exams	
	8. F.E. Evening at school	
	9. Interview with Careers Officer	
	10. Hand-in dates for course work	
	11. GCSE exams	
	12. Apply for FE/6th form	
	13. Open Evenings at Post	
	14. Closing date for post-16 book applications	
	15. GCSE results out	
	16. Get Opportunities Post 16 Booklet	
	17. Last day at school	
	18. Interview for FE/6th form	
	19. Apply for employment/training	
	20. Check vacancies notified by Careers Centre	
	21. Parents Evening	
	22. Careers group work planning sessions	
	23. Information session with Careers Officer	
	24. Visit Careers Library to find out more	
	25. Draft C.V. (curriculum vitae)	

Table 3.8 is an extract from a residential experience diary It incorporates the elements of recording and planning. Table 3.9 offers a series of extracts from a more free-form diary and planner. The extracts include a weekly homework record, a termly Record of Achievement, a term planner and a blank proforma for recording the year's targets.

Table 3.10 comes from Cambridgeshire Careers Service. It offers a list of key events for year 11 pupils and a planner to enable them to organise themselves throughout this transitional year. Students in other years may find this type of key-event list helpful in order to plan their personal and academic lives.

These types of vehicles for recording information will assist young people when they engage with IAP and try to set themselves targets.

Planning

Some young people are resistant to the notion of planning their time and argue that it stops or slows them down. Some feel planning means timetables, and some feel that it is not possible to plan for the future, but that life has a happenchance quality.

The adult working with young people will have to offer good reasons for planning, which is more likely to solicit young people's co-operation and interest than simply dictating that planning is 'a good idea'. Teachers might rehearse some of the positive properties, of planning, a few of which are listed below.

Planning helps young people to:

1. Have a clear understanding and vision of what they want and need to do and why they are doing it. This saves time by avoiding unnecessary tasks.
2. Think about alternative courses of action and make judgements in terms of consequences, outcomes and resources. This encourages greater self-awareness and an awareness of the implications of actions.
3. Decide how to reach their goal. This engenders a greater sense of being in control.
4. Increase their chances of succeeding in reaching their goal.
5. Give them a measure against which they can determine their progress and successes, by offering a structure of short, medium- and long-term goals.
6. Know why they may abandon a task, why something is no longer appropriate or where something is failing. This gives them a sense of greater control over events and self-esteem rather than a sense of simply failing to complete something.

7. Consider potential problems and generate a range of solutions which can be activated if needed.

The consequences of not planning prior to starting a task or embarking upon a course of action can be deleterious and disruptive to its successful completion. Young people setting out on an activity without forethought may be unsure of what they are really trying to do, unsure of what constitutes success, unaware of the consequences of their actions and unaware of the possible problems they may meet.

At the outset of work on planning, young people will consider their broad goals. Ultimately they will move towards detailed targets.However, in the early stages of planning determining a broad goal may well be difficult enough. Often young people have little sense of themselves as being able to effect changes or of being in control of what they do.Young people need to be trained to devise clear aims, to determine how to realise a goal and to know when they have succeeded.

In the previous sections on raising self-awareness and thinking about time there were some exercises which encouraged thinking about currently held qualities, skills or practices and the ways in which these might be developed. These exercises can be a starting point for goal formulation.

Aside from self-awareness raising materials, there are occasions when broad aims naturally suggest themselves, at, for example, points of transition, such as moving into senior school, at the close of a module of work or at a yearly review. At this stage, by reviewing and thinking about the future a number of tasks may suggest themselves. Tables 3.11–3.14 have been taken from schools and colleges, as pupils move from primary to secondary school and to review progress.

Table 3.11

MY PRIMARY SCHOOL

SECONDARY SCHOOL

WHAT AM I LOOKING FORWARD TO

MY RESPONSIBILITIES

WHAT I SHALL TRY TO DO AT SECONDARY SCHOOL

AWARDS I HAVE EARNED

SIGNED _____
DATE _____

SCHOOL CLUBS AND TEAMS
I HAVE BEEN IN

PRESENTATIONS I HAVE BEEN IN

Table 3.12

FIRST YEAR RECORD OF ACHIEVEMENT
PERSONAL SOCIAL QUALITIES / SKILLS

ENTHUSIASM

I offer to do something	
I am a regular helper	
I expect things to go well	
I take an active part	
I am a good trier and a keen worker	

ENTERPRISE

I think and act for myself, I start work without being told	
I ask questions	
I am a good organiser of work	
I make a great effort	
I take a chance when it is offered	
I have exciting new ideas	

ADAPTABILITY

I am willing to change	
I am prepared to consider other opinions and ideas	
I obey rules	
I am able to use skills in different situations, I show common sense	

PERSISTENCE

I do not give up or lose heart	
I am prepared to tackle difficult situations	

PUNCTUALITY

I am always on time	
I do jobs/tasks straight away	
I return letters/slips on time, bring notes on time	

WILLINGNESS

I listen carefully to instructions and to what others say	
I am keen to join in	
I look for work and for responsibilities	
I encourage and support others	

Table 3.13

4th YEAR RECORD OF ACHIEVEMENT: PERSONAL STATEMENT

*Write an outline of what you understand to have been your strengths
and weaknesses throughout the year in all aspects of your school life.
Include some realistic, achievable personal goals to aim for over the
next twelve months*

_____

_____

_____

_____

_____

_____

_____

_____

_____

_____

_____

_____

_____

_____

_____

_____

_____

_____

_____

_____

_____

Table 3.14 Blackburn College – Record of Achievement. Self achievement sheet

---

NAME: SUBJECT:

Use the following questions to help you assess your progress to date:

What grade do you need to achieve in order to
follow your chosen career path?

What are your main strengths in this subject?

What do you find difficult?

Have you got better or worse in areas of this subject? (Give details)

How much time do you spend on this
subject outside of class?

What else have you done outside class to improve your understanding of the
subject?

How do you organize your notes?

How do you revise for tests and exams?

Anything else you wish to add?

The following check-list can be used at any time to assist young people to take stock of their current position. They can ask themselves questions such as:
- Where am I now?
- Am I happy in my current position?

- Do I have goals that I should like to achieve?
- How close am I to succeeding in what I want to do?
- Could I make myself an opportunity to change what I am doing?
- Where do I want to be?
- Do I have any long-term aims?
- What are they?
- How close am I to doing what I should like to in the long-term?

Once young people have identified a global aim or aims, found some discrepancy between where they should like to be and where they currently stand, the time is ripe to introduce more detailed planning.

Section 3: Setting Actionable Targets

Many young people find target setting difficult. Problems arise when they move from a broad aim towards actionable targets. Often their aims are insufficiently well-focused and the creation of realistic and, therefore, actionable steps need practice.

Young people need to address the following questions as an aid to their planning.

Ask yourself:
- what do I want to do?

- What does this mean to me?

- Why do I want to do it?

- Where am I now?

- How far am I from my goals?

- How can I get to where I want to be?

- What do I need to achieve my aim?

- Who else can help me do this?

- By when do I want to achieve my aim?

At this stage young people could try a planning and goal setting exercise, such as that shown in Table 3.15. It may help highlight the planning process before students embark upon setting their own targets.

Table 3.15 (Produced by Oldham Careers Service.)

PLANNING
INSTRUCTION SHEET FOR STUDENTS: THE SMALL GROUP ACTIVITY
Please write the names of the students in the group:

1........................2.............................3...........................

4........................5.............................6...........................

Choose one of the following activities which you would be willing to organise:
A Sports Competition / A day or evening activity for a residential / A fund raising activity for charity / An out of School/College activity / An application for a place at the sixth form college.
(UNDERLINE THE ONE THE GROUP CHOOSES)

Write down all the jobs that would have to be done to arrange the activity you have chosen.
(DO IT AS A BRAINSTORM WHERE ONE PERSON WRITES DOWN ALL THE IDEAS OFFERED BY ANYONE IN THE GROUP AND IN ANY ORDER.)

Look at the ideas and follow this action planning process.
What do we want to do?

How do we want to do it?

Who do we need to consult?

Are there any other ways of doing it?

How do we choose the best way?

In what order do we need to carry out the tasks?

Who is in charge of doing each task?

At this stage it should be reiterated that breaking the goal into smaller units of action and attempting only one or two at a time will be the only way to achieve the longer-term goal. This can be illustrated thus:

Target 1: to be sure to take the right things to school. (Figures 3.5 and 3.6).

Figure 3.5 Aim: to be more organised at school.

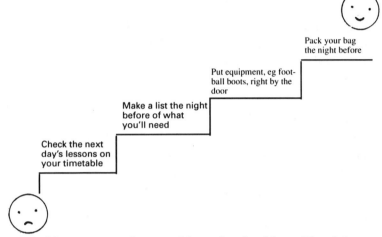

Figure 3.6 Aim: to get on better with my brother/sister. Try *doing* some of these things and then discuss with your teacher or a friend how you've got on. Did these actions help?

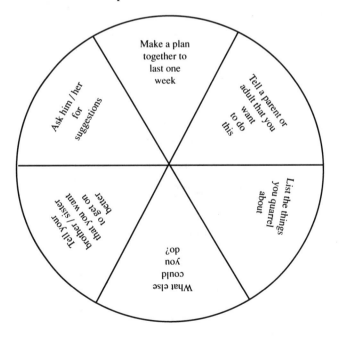

Young people need to be taught to set themselves:

- a realisable goal, with
- smaller targets to reach *en route.*

These targets have to be:

- timebound
- clearly understood
- things which the young person can do and wants to do
- seen to be contributing to the overall goal
- structured sequentially, if necessary
- measurable against pre-defined and understood criteria.

Young people need to be taught to take responsibility for checking their own progress towards completing their targets and not to rely on others. They need to be clear about the criteria against which they are checking their progress and become habituated in monitoring their own activities.

The following very basic plans shown in Tables 3.16 and 3.17 can be used to help young people negotiate this stage and instil some of the processes for creating effective targets.

Table 3.16

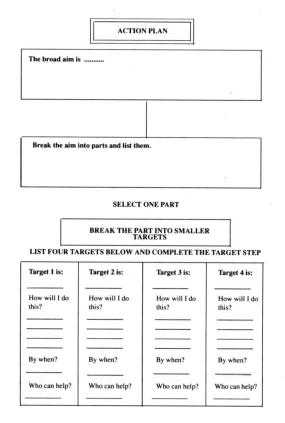

Table 3.17

```
┌─────────────────────────────┐
│        ACTION PLAN          │
└─────────────────────────────┘
```

This is what I can do now:

This is what I would like to do:

To do this I need to:

The steps to completing my plan are:
i)

ii)

iii)

iv)

My plan is to do:

i)   by _____   ii)   by _____
iii)   by _____   iv)   by _____

Section IV: Reviewing Progress towards Goals.

The skills of raising self-awareness, planning, monitoring progress and reviewing are complementary and mutually reinforcing. This should be explained to young people so that they are better able to appreciate the value of investing their time in developing such skills and the multiple returns on their investment. In developing their skills young people will become more effective planners. Through reviewing their progress, they will become more efficient in the types of target setting they do and in the time scales they set for themselves. The whole review process can be outlined as shown in Figure 3.7.

Adults undertaking review activities with young people will need basic counselling skills and strategies. These were outlined in Chapter 2 and are in more detail in Chapter 7. As with all stages of IAP, adults need to know why they are asking young people to engage in review. Many young people feel that simply completing an action or task is sufficient in itself and balk at further reflection and discussion, and at the discipline required to determine what they have learnt from their experiences. Young people need to be made aware that reviewing gives them an opportunity to:

- evaluate their performance and progress
- think further about themselves
- think about alternative ways of completing what they had undertaken
- work out what could be taken from the learning experience and used to good effect in subsequent ones.

A note about evidence

Young people will need help in developing their own success criteria and in determining the nature and type of evidence which can help them evaluate their achievements. Most young people will have been used to others determining their successes and failures. Thus, being asked to take responsibility for collecting, interpreting and presenting the evidence which demonstrates their progress will be alien to many young people. Many will feel reticent and be underconfident about suggesting what they have achieved. Others may be all too easily impressed by their own success and fail really to evaluate the grounds on which they base their claims. These young people will have to be helped to consider critically the quality of evidence they select and the validity of their judgements. They will need to be aware of a range of standards and of the possibilities of being able to improve upon their own earlier benchmarks of achievement.

It will take skilful tutoring to encourage pupils to evaluate the evidence they have collected but which may be of poorer quality than the pupils thought. Although young people are to be encouraged to be in charge of their personal development they have to develop an understanding of standards and develop their own.

Building from the review session

The review session should allow young people to create a bridge between their understandings of their past experiences and choices, and their future actions and decisions. At the close of a review session young people should make informed decisions about their next course of action and its execution. They should have evaluated their previous actions and ways of working and behaving, and determine whether to reject or maintain them.

This chapter has offered a range of exercises which can help teaching staff and young people develop the latter's skills more effectively to undertake the IAP process.

Figure 3.7

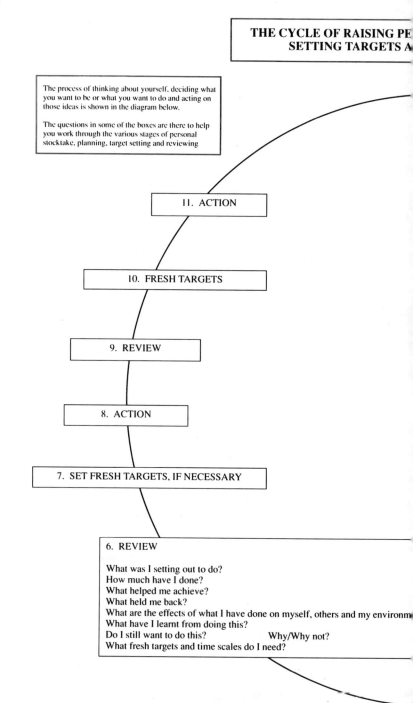

THE CYCLE OF RAISING PE
SETTING TARGETS A

The process of thinking about yourself, deciding what you want to be or what you want to do and acting on those ideas is shown in the diagram below.

The questions in some of the boxes are there to help you work through the various stages of personal stocktake, planning, target setting and reviewing

11. ACTION

10. FRESH TARGETS

9. REVIEW

8. ACTION

7. SET FRESH TARGETS, IF NECESSARY

6. REVIEW

What was I setting out to do?
How much have I done?
What helped me achieve?
What held me back?
What are the effects of what I have done on myself, others and my environm
What have I learnt from doing this?
Do I still want to do this?   Why/Why not?
What fresh targets and time scales do I need?

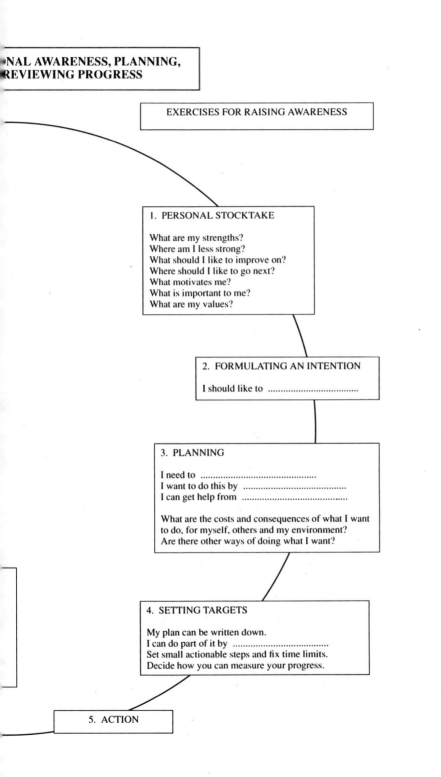

NAL AWARENESS, PLANNING,
REVIEWING PROGRESS

EXERCISES FOR RAISING AWARENESS

1. PERSONAL STOCKTAKE

What are my strengths?
Where am I less strong?
What should I like to improve on?
Where should I like to go next?
What motivates me?
What is important to me?
What are my values?

2. FORMULATING AN INTENTION

I should like to ....

3. PLANNING

I need to ....
I want to do this by ....
I can get help from ....

What are the costs and consequences of what I want
to do, for myself, others and my environment?
Are there other ways of doing what I want?

4. SETTING TARGETS

My plan can be written down.
I can do part of it by ....
Set small actionable steps and fix time limits.
Decide how you can measure your progress.

5. ACTION

4 Individual Action Plans

Introduction

This chapter addresses the documentation which emerges from the processes of IAP, the Individual Action Plan. There are two main types of Plan: private, formative working documents and Action Plans which enter the public domain, usually at times of transition. The chapter describes both types of documentation and offers examples of each. It offers a series of issues to be considered by staff involved in designing Action Plans. Finally the chapter describes some of the benefits of having Individual Action Plans.

Individual Action Plans

An Action Plan will contain some personal details such as:

- the individual's name;
- recent educational, training or work experience;
- a record of any qualifications or awards undertaken, either wholly or partially completed.

It will contain information on the individual's goals and learning needs to reach such goals.

The Action Plan may, depending on its purpose and audience, include a range of possible goals and information on personal interests and plans, personal development needs, learning routes and preferred learning, training or employment outcomes. Formative Action Plans may include personal targets.

All Action Plans should include a review date, as it is part of an ongoing process of development and assessment. The Plan, whatever its proposed uses, can never be treated as a terminal statement of an individual's intentions. The IAP may change as a person reflects on his or her current needs, experiences, aspirations and achievements. Further factors extrinsic to the person such as the nature of the local labour market, the availability and types of education and training provision will also influence an individual's aspirations and plans.

The contents of the Individual Action Plan will be determined by the age of the young person, the stage which they have reached in their school or college careers, and the proposed uses of the Individual Action Plan. The differences between the two main types of Plan – formative Plans and Individual Action Plans at transition – are outlined below.

Formative Individual Action Plans

These Action Plans should be treated as confidential to the young person. They *function as working documents* and as such may explore a range of potential personal and occupational options, contain targets to meet learning and information needs, and identify areas for personal development. As private documents the individual does not have to self-censor nor pretend to knowledge. The entries can be as explicit as the individual finds useful. These Plans can afford to be testing, tentative and reasonably wide-ranging. Attention can be given to exploring ideas and aspirations rather than to considering issues of presentation.

Individual Action Plans at Transition

Unlike the formative Plans, Action Plans at transition are documents for the public arena. Young people should be aware of the difference in function between the two types of IAP. Plans at transition are likely to hold more limited and less personal information. Taking account of the proposed audience they may offer few occupational options. Indeed, there may be more than one Action Plan, each aimed at different audiences. As documents which may be used during interviews, attention has to be paid to presentation, clarity of expression and technical accuracy in addition to quality of content. They will probably include a statement of vocational or educational aims, training needs and the individual's action steps.

These documents may be used by the young person to negotiate entry to a subsequent phase of education or training or when moving within the employment market. These Plans can enable the individual to ask more clearly for what he or she wants or needs from a future employer, trainer or educator and form the basis for developing further training, education or professional development plans. Figures 4.1–4.9 show both types of Plan.

Figure 4.1 Manchester Compact. Pupil Individual Action Plan.
Personal Information

NAME

DATE OF BIRTH   /   /   FEMALE/MALE (delete)

HOME ADDRESS

Post Code   Telephone

SCHOOL   FORM

COURSES FOLLOWED	LEVEL (GCSE. UNIT CREDIT. ETC.)

Figure 4.2 Personal Development

Favourite school subjects	
Other school activities	
Position(s) of responsibility In School	Out of School
Work experience (position and dates)	Part-time employment (position and dates)
Career ideas including Further Education	

58

Figure 4.3 Manchester Compact Action Plan

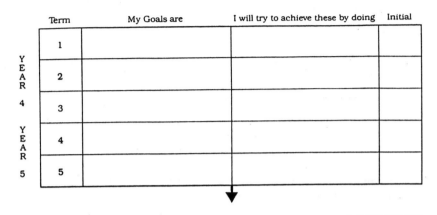

	Term	My Goals are	I will try to achieve these by doing	Initial
Y E A R 4	1			
	2			
	3			
Y E A R 5	4			
	5			

Other ideas I have discussed with my careers teacher / officer are:

Signed   Date

	Term	Present	Aim	Achieved by	Signed by
ATTENDANCE TARGETS	1				
	2				
	3				
	4				
	5				
PUNCTUALITY TARGETS	1				
	2				
	3				
	4				
	5				

I have discussed my plan with my teachers and will bring my action plan with me to each review.
I have set myself other targets in subject and cross curricular areas.

Student Signature .... Date ....

Parent/Guardian .... Signed on behalf of school ....

Countersigned by Employer's Representative ....

Figure 4.4 Individual Action Plan (Careers Training Action Plan, Lincoln Careers)

MY PRESENT SITUATION

Skills, Experience of work, Personal qualities, Achievements (school, abilities, aptitudes), Mobility (physical health, transport), Financial situation (benefits), Previous jobs/training schemes applied for, Social and domestic circumstances, Other organisations involved (Social Services, Probation etc).

WHAT DO I WANT TO DO ?	HOW DO I ACHIEVE THIS ?	include timescales involved

Figure 4.5 Individual Action Plan, continued

WHAT DO I WANT TO DO ? cont'd	HOW DO I ACHIEVE THIS ? cont'd
	include timescales involved

In job / training aim, Reasons for choice, Qualifications aimed at, Additional vocational interests, Skills aimed at, Experiences aimed at, Skills / Experience, Qualifications to be improved

WHAT HELP DO I NEED ?

WHO – Training organisations, Employers, Tutors, Careers Service, TEC   WHAT –. Transport, Specialist equipment, Educational help, Confidence building, Counselling, Supervision, Development of personal skills, Reviewing systems.

ADDITIONAL ACTION POINTS / ANY OTHER COMMENTS

Review dates, Applications, Long term targets, People to be involved in future reviews.

Signed _____   Date _____

_____   _____

Figure 4.6

COMPACT GOALS
How are you getting on?
Summer review Year 10

Oldham COMPACT

OLDHAM
CAREERS
SERVICE

<u>Attendance</u>

Getting 90% or above? _____ *Well done* if you are.

If not, why not? _____

How can you improve? _____

<u>Punctuality</u>

Getting 90% or above? _____ *Well done* if you are.

If not, why not? _____

How can you improve? _____

<u>Behaviour</u>

Are you sticking to the rules of the school? _____ *Well done* if you are.

If not, why not? _____

How can you improve? _____

<u>Schoolwork</u>

Are you and your teachers satisfied with your work in your subjects? _____ *Well done.*

If not, why not? _____

How can you improve? _____

<u>Work Experience</u>

You might have been out on work experience this term.

Have you met your COMPACT work experience target? _____ *Well done* if you have.

If not, why not? _____

<u>Targets for the next term</u>

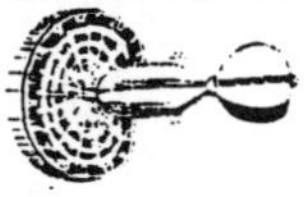

Keep up the good work - you are *on target* for success.

If you're not on target try to improve these things. _____

_____

Figure 4.7 End of Year 10 Action Checklist (Oldham YDP Compact Action Plan)

Oldham COMPACT

OLDHAM
CAREERS
SERVICE

One career I am considering is:

My next steps at the end of Year 11 could be:

I have spoken to
and/or have found out that:

The qualifications/grades I need are:

The skills I need/would be useful are:

I need to apply to:

Other things I need to do are:

*

*

One career I am considering is:

My next steps at the end of Year 11 could be:

I have spoken to
and/or have found out that:

The qualifications/grades I need are:

The skills I need/would be useful are:

I need to apply to:

Other things I need to do are:

*

*

Figure 4.8

Current Action Plan of

My goals for the future are
(i.e. Education, employment/training, other goals)

What I will need to achieve these goals
(e.g. Skills, abilities, qualifications to be achieved)

Signed   Date

Figure 4.9

INDIVIDUAL ACTION PLAN	
The following statement has been written by the student in consultation with other people	

Name	Henry Hampshire

What I have done

I am currently completing the second year of my BTEC National Diploma in Business and Finance. I have also paid for and had trials for a numerous amount of professional clubs.

What I have got to do

I am going to sign onto 3 or 4 agencies in the city for insurance reinsurance etc. I am also going to have trials with professional clubs all around the country in the hope that I can become a professional footballer.

What I want to do

I want to be a pro footballer if not I would like to own my own business. But what ever I do I am going to be successful.

Signature		Date	
Name		Position	
Signature		Date	

The Content, Style and Format of Action Plans

The Plan should be the product of a comprehensive guidance process. It should be owned and controlled by the individual to whom it relates and should only reflect the young person's interests, achievements and aims. It should be a document which is comprehensible to the young person and which, with training, he or she is able to use. The completion of the Plan should not be the focus of the IAP session but a record of the process.

In some instances a format for Action Plans will be locally determined, for example those which accompany Training Credits. The following pages consider situations where tutors have latitude in devising Action Planning documents.

Devising Action Plans

A number of issues have to be considered when creating Action Plans so that they meet the needs of the full range of young people which the institution serves. Staff may decide that one Plan cannot meet all individuals' needs and so they may create several versions. In producing IAP documentation tutors will need to ask themselves questions such as those which follow below.

Of its format:
- How long should it be?
- Should it be question-driven or blank?
- What is meant by quality documentation?
- What of Special Needs young people?
- Is text always appropriate and what alternatives might there be?

Of its content:
- What should be the balance between academic, vocational and personal concerns?
- What should be the balance between recording past achievements and future targets?

Teachers may also consider how young people can be involved in developing their own Action Plan formats. Staff should think about the match between the age of the young person, the uses of the Plan, the information it contains and its style of presentation.

When creating documentation, staff will need to determine how the information recorded on the Plan will complement other assessment documents or whether a house style has to be adopted.

Figures 4.10 and 4.11 show some examples of Action Plans. These Plans show the range from a questionnaire to an almost blank sheet.

Figure 4.12 is an example of the use of symbols in answering Action Planning questions. As described in the previous chapter, the young person makes use of a mouse to take symbols from a symbol bank and enter them on his or her IAP sheet. The use of symbols either commercially produced or created through a scanner enables young people with severe learning difficulties to record autonomously their experiences and ideas. Other formats such as video and audio tape can be used with special education and training needs young people.

Completing and Accessing Individual Action Plans

Having spent time devising Action Plans, perhaps in negotiation with

Figure 4.10

```
                    ┌─────────────────────────┐
                    │  INDIVIDUAL ACTION PLAN  │
        NAME:       └─────────────────────────┘


        AIM(S)




        NEEDS:




        ACTION STEPS:




        Signature: ─────────────────          Date: ─────────
        Signature: ───────────── Position: ───────────── Date: ─────────
```

students, tutors will then work with them during the course of the IAP process. This stage creates another series of issues which have to be addressed.

Young people receive many messages about the IAP process, the value of the Plan and how they themselves are regarded from the ways in which

Figure 4.11

INDIVIDUAL ACTION PLAN

NAME: DATE:

SCHOOL AND SUBJECTS
1. Of the subjects that I am studying I prefer:

2. What makes them interesting:

3. I know in schoolwork I am good at:

4. This is because:

5. Ideas, concepts and skills gained:

6. I least enjoy:

OUT OF SCHOOL PURSUITS
7. (a) I think out of school I use my time well/badly because:

I could use it more effectively if:

If I could I should like to:

(b) What I enjoy most about the out of school activities which I do undertake are:

Doing these things gives me:

The aspects of these activities whcih I would most like to pursue are:

LIFESTYLE
8. The things which are most important to me in my life at the moment are:

9. When I think about my life when i am older I think the following things
will be important to me:

THINKING ABOUT THE FUTURE
10. When I think about the jobs and careers which people do I am most
interested in:

11. because

Figure 4.11 continued

12. I think my understanding of the possible jobs/careers which are available to me is good/fair/bad:

13. I think the skills involved in these are:

14. I can improve my understanding by:

15. For my work experience I would like to undertake:

because:

16. Looking back on my answers to schoolwork, hobbies and interests, my lifestyle and possible job areas. I think these aspects fit well/badly:
    This is because:

17. I think my own strengths and skills are:

18. I think that this discussion about myself and my interests has been:

19. To make the next one useful I think I need to think about:

20. Between now and the next meeting I would like to:

SIGNATURE:
DATE:

the Action Plan is completed during IAP sessions. The Plan may emerge from one or several Planning sessions during which the young person has explored ideas or the Plan may have dominated the session, so that completion of the document seemed the sole purpose of the session. Such differing approaches will convey very different messages to the young action planners.

In completing a Plan, a number of issues need to be addressed.

In producing the plan:
- Who writes the plan and why is it that person?
- Is the Plan signed?
- What do such signatures mean?
- Is the final form of the Plan a written text?
- How will the Plan be finally produced?
- What is suggested to the young person and end-users by having a well-produced document?

- Should IT packages be used to create the Plan?
- What are the effects of using statement banks?

Of copies, access and storage it needs to be asked:
- How many copies of the Plan will there be?
- Will the young person have a copy?
- Who else will have copies?
- How will the Plans be stored?
- How often can the Plans be updated?

Finally:
- What is the relationship of the IAP document to RoA, NRA and other forms of reporting in school/college?
- What is the relationship between the Plan and Careers Service Summaries of Guidance?
- What is the status of the Plan?
- Is the Plan a working document or a contract?

Figure 4.12 Plan from St. Francis School, Lincoln

Date **12/2/92** _____

Personal achievements
Sports

 500 metres

To some extent these issues may be determined by practical considerations or constraints on resources, for example the institution may not be able to afford to word-process all Plans, or young people themselves may not have easy access to IT equipment. Practicalities notwithstanding, the issues outlined above should be addressed, for each indicates the seriousness with which the institution holds individual young people and their futures.

The following pages explore some of the questions outlined above, as an aid to staff debate. The list is far from exhaustive.

Who writes the Plan and Why?

Writing the Plan can be a thorny issue. Some young people may not enjoy writing and prefer the adult to produce a summary of their discussions. However, others may like to keep their own record in their own language. There are dangers that in an adult scribe taking over the sessions because it is quicker than allowing young people to write for themselves. Adults may engage in censorship, leaving out aspects of the discussions which they do not approve of or which they feel will disadvantage the young person. When young people write their IAPs, adults may suggest what the young person should write to quicken the process or to add a gloss to what the young person commits to paper.

A fundamental principle of the Action Plan is that nothing should be written on the Plan with which the young person disagrees. Adults need to be aware that their choice of words, expressions or omissions can misrepresent what is said in the IAP session.

Should the Plan be a Written Document?

Although a written document can be a useful *aide mémoire*, there is clearly little point if the language is alien to the young person, the print too small or the level of literacy too high. Other forms of recording and of final presentation to end-users may need to be found.

Arguments are advanced for the importance of a quality-produced document as it enhances the status of the Plan in the eyes of the young person and possible end-users. However, if quality intimidates the young person from writing on or amending the Action Plan then it has lost its function as a working document. It may not be so much the quality of the document but the ways in which documentation is used which will impress young people and end-users. Quality production may satisfy an institution's self-image but could result in the young person seeing the Plan as being little more than just another piece of documentation.

What does signing the Plan mean?

Opinion differs about the merits of signing the Plan. It is worth questioning what signing the document means.

- Does signing indicate that the young person has gone through a particular process?
- If so, what is that process?
- Will it be common across a school or college in its format, regularity and quality?
- Who would monitor this?
- Does signing suggest that the young person is going to do all the things on the Plan?
- Does this mean the Plan has the status of a contract?
- If so, what happens if the young person does not complete all their targets?
- Does signing by an adult suggest that he or she is party to the completion of the Plan, to doing something to help the young person or to monitoring progress?

These questions may be a useful starting point for staff discussion. In part such questions may be answered by the intended use of the Plan, the institution's available resources for meeting IAP and the extent to which an institution is able to countenance and to foster the individual empowerment of young people.

Copies, storage, access and revisions

Clearly, young people should be informed of institutional decisions about the number of copies of Plans which are produced, how they are stored and who has access to them. As the Plan belongs to the individual to whom it relates, not giving young people their Plans in case they lose them is hard to support.

Young people may want to revise to their Plans in between planning and review sessions. They will need to know if this is possible. They will also need to know about formal review sessions and their frequency.

Integration of the Plan with other forms of assessment and recording

There will be guidance from TECs about the development of IAP processes and documentation in schools and colleges and integration with Training Credits. Similarly, the National Council for Vocational Qualifications is preparing guidance on Plans and their integration with the NRA.

The Benefit of the Written Action Plan

There are several groups who benefit from the written Plan: the young person, teachers or tutors, careers advisers and end-users such as employees, trainers or admissions tutors.

Young people find it useful to have a written Plan. It acts as a record of past achievements, future goals and personal development and learning routes. The documentation of time-bound targets means the Plan is a tool against which they can check their own progress. The Plan clearly sets out the young person's possible options and the ways to action such options, which minimises confusion and creates a sense of the young person being in control of his or her future. The written document helps to legitimise and formalise goals and aspirations and shows young people how they may be realised.

The document is a store of information which can be used in completing application forms and as a record of personal development. The Plan helps demonstrate to young people that they and their futures are being taken seriously. Finally, the written document can become a useful tool when the young person is approaching employers, trainers or other gatekeepers of their futures.

Teachers, tutors and careers officers also gain from the written IAP. The Plan:

- allows young people's progress to be monitored;
- is a useful tool to facilitate and focus discussion;
- is a full record of ideas, intentions and aspirations which can later be reconsidered in the light of action.

The document is a store of information about past achievements and experiences. For adult planning partners as for young people this can assist when discussing future choices or creating reports about the young person. The written document enables teaching staff and careers officers to have access to students' prior experiences, learning and development.

Some careers officers have found that the written Plan serves as a bridge between school and college activities and choices post-16 or post-18. It is a clear statement of how the young person would wish to proceed. For end-users, the written Plan at transition is a starting point for discussion about the young person's future plans, intentions and requirements. This can enhance the possibilities of appropriately matching a young person with training or employment opportunities, thereby reducing personal and institutionally expensive 'drop out', disappointment and frustration.

For these various gains to be made from having the written Plan, young people, the adult planning partners and a range of end-users need to be trained in its use and the meaning of the Plan.

Using the Individual Action Plan

Tutors and young people need to make use of the series of working formative IAP documents which are produced through successive IAP discussions. Each document should build on previous ones. The series of documents will be a vast store of information and young people and adults need to know how to analyse the information so as to tease out:

- how ideas have evolved;
- how skills have been developed;
- what ideas have been tested and with what result;
- what can be understood about young people's ability to realise targets and what future help might be useful;
- what qualities, competences and skills the young person has developed;
- how recent ideas and aims have come about and how realistic they are in the light of earlier experience.

Questions will need to be broadly focused and open-ended. The tutor may also consider letting the young person drive the discussion, selecting what is to be addressed and which aspects of earlier Plans would most usefully be reviewed.

Tutors may prepare briefing sheets for young people to encourage them to think both about their formative and transitional Action Plans. Two examples of such documents are shown in Figures 4.13 and 4.14.

Young people and the recipients of Action Plans need to be taught about using the Plan at interviews, be they employment or training interviews or an end of year review. It is essential that young people do not try to use their Plan as a substitute for presenting themselves and trying to negotiate what they want. Similarly the adult end-user must not see the Plan as an additional piece of evidence in a selection process or endow with too much significance simply because it is a document and may be easier to deal with than the young person. Recipients will also need to be alerted to the importance of linking subsequent education, training or employment provision to the needs identified in the Action Plan and to using the Plan as a basis for subsequent ones.

Figure 4.13 Youth Development project. Action Plan – User's Guide (Cambridge Careers Service YDP)

* It's yours
* You decide whether anyone else sees it or actually reads it

* You decide if and when it might help you

* You choose which parts if any to use

Your Action Plan:

* Highlights your good points and relevant experiences

* Outlines your short and longer term plans

* Give reasons for your choices

* Focuses on what others might expect of you

* Lists other things for you to do

When you might use it:

* At interviews – for further education, college, employment, training

* As a prompt sheet to remind you of things done and to do

* As a basis for future planning

N.B. Action Plans are only relevant for a limited period depending upon your plans and your circumstances. A new action plan should be drawn up when you make a change.

Figure 4.14 Guidelines for Students. How to use your Action Plan (Newcastle YDP)

During the last year, you have been working through the Action Planning Pack with your tutor

This has helped you look at your strengths and weaknesses, your interests and abilities, and your skills and experience.

You will also have set yourself some targets for the future – achievements qualifications or career goals for which you are aiming.

These are now brought together on your Action Plan. This sets out your goals, and the steps you need to take to achieve them. It is your 'shopping list' of what you want to do or achieve next.

Other people will be interested in the information and ideas your Action Plan contains, for example –

- an **employer** when interviewing you for a job
- a **college admissions tutor** when discussing your application for a course
- a **Youth Training Provider** who may have the right training opportunities for you
- your **Careers Officer**, who can help you make decisions about the options and choices you have

The Action Plan belongs to you, and you decide how you are going to use it, and who to show it to. However, employers etc. know how Action Plans are developed, and may expect to see yours at interviews. So, when you are writing yours, think about –

- Will it help you get what you want? If it says you want to be a nurse, but are applying for a secretarial job, it won't help your chances.
- Is it up-to-date? If you have changed your mind, you may need to see your careers officer again to discuss your options.
- Does it give the right impression of you and your interests?

Your tutor will have an example of a completed Action Plan to illustrate the sort of things you might include.

Read through your Action Plan and decide how you want to use it. You may wish to keep some of your goals private, and share others. Don't forget, as your plans change, as you get different qualifications, experience and targets, your Action Plan should be updated.

5 The Principles of Action Planning

Introduction

This chapter addresses some of the rhetoric surrounding IAP, much of which is expressed as principles for effective and quality IAP. An understanding of these principles and their implication is important for institutions to determine the impact of developing IAP within particular educational or training context.

The following principles are explored.

1. The IAP process is more important than the product.
2. IAP empowers the individual.
3. IAP is done with, not done to, the individual.
4. The individual should have access to plentiful, impartial and comprehensive counselling.
5. The individual has ownership of the Individual Action Plan.
6. Nothing should be placed on an individual's Action Plan with which he or she does not agree.
7. IAP is an on-going process of target setting, review and evaluation.

These principles have implications for the ways in which the learners' roles are conceived and for resourcing IAP. If Action Plans are to be acted upon then there will be systemic implications for the type of education or training offered and styles of delivery.

Process before Product

One of the tenets of IAP is that the process is of greater significance than the Product. The reasons for this are severalfold. Individual Action Planning allows the young person to explore past achievements, prior learning and experiences, interests, qualities and skills. The process of making these elements explicit to another helps the learner raise their own self-awareness and enables the individual and the adult to detect patterns or perceive qualities of which the individual may hitherto have been unaware.

In exploring the young person's past and present the Planning discussions may uncover reasons why certain earlier courses of action have been abandoned and identify ways in which earlier achievements can be built upon. This groundwork creates solid foundations for the subsequent consideration of the young person's development, be it personal, social, educational or vocational.

Discussing what the young person has undertaken in a positive way helps cement the IAP relationship and boost the individual's self-esteem. A realisation of what has been achieved is a powerful tool for helping the young person appreciate what might be undertaken and achieved in future.

If the planning partner, ignoring the young person's past, launched into a discussion of what could be done next then there may be a risk of the learner setting unrealisable and unrealistic targets.

In the context of open discussion the young person is invited to be tentative, to focus on possible achievements and to request help or information. In such a supportive context the young person may feel that aspirations which previously had the quality of fantasies could be feasible.

The process of exploring the past and discussing the future can help an individual with little sense of what his or her future is. Although people cannot be forced to take action, nor should they be pressurised to accept another's targets, the IAP process can give a young person ideas and insights. Effective referrals can help the young person to explore new areas and to tease out any which seem fraught.

In summary, the process, based upon impartial and attentive counselling, is an important one. Through the process young people can:

- raise their self-awareness;
- talk about themselves;
- table their concerns;
- explore areas of conflict;
- explore aspirations;
- be enabled to determine their information needs;
- be taught to analyse information;
- be encouraged to understand the decision-making process;
- be encouraged to think of themselves as problem-solvers and as instigators of action in their own lives.

Through the process, the product, the individual's Action Plan, becomes a commitment to paper of longer-term goals and immediate action steps. The Plan is informed by the individual's previous experiences and the targets thoughtfully framed and the means to realise them fully discussed.

Partnership, Empowerment and Access

Partnerships

The Action Planning partners need to be trained to meet the demands of their respective roles. If the training has been successful both adult and young person should appreciate that they work from the outset in a managed partnership. IAP sessions overturn a number of socialised role expectations. The young person has to uncouple from dependency on the adult's approval and a need for adults to direct and suggest. The young person has to learn to stand firm and not feel that his or her ideas, concerns or strategies are invalid or of little worth.

The tutor has to accept that the young person has insight, self-knowledge and an appreciation of what might be most appropriate. Only if both learner and tutor challenge their pre-conceptions of appropriate roles will there be a partnership which allows a learning process rather than a situation in which IAP is done to the student and which confirms each in their traditional roles.

Empowerment

Action Planning processes placing the student at its centre should be empowering. However, the student will not feel empowered if he or she does not know how to deal with the situation and is floundering over what may happen next.

Adults involved in IAP work need to explain why IAP is taking place within the institution, to rehearse roles and expectations, and to chart out the process. Throughout various sessions young people need to be told what is on the adult's agenda for discussion, why this should be so and that he or she can add to this.

Young people may also find IAP empowering if they are permitted by the institution to be proactive about who they plan with, how frequently and for how long. Young people will feel naturally drawn to certain teaching staff, and in some institutions or where smaller scale IAP work takes place, it may be possible to allow such free choice. Decisions about the timing of IAP and review sessions may be determined more by institutional constraints than the young person's need.

Finally, part of the empowering quality of IAP is that it should be an educative process. It should allow young people to develop such transferable competences as time and personal management, the skills to collect and interpret information and decision making. The process should encourage young people to understand and become familiar with the language of learning and training, thereby placing them on a more equal footing with such providers. Young people should be able to ask for provision and to determine whether their needs are being met.

Access

Much of what empowers young people is access to quality and comprehensive guidance processes, and to wide-ranging and current information. Access to human resources should allow young people to make greater sense of any information they collect and to make realistic choices for themselves.

The type and quality of information to which young people have access is determined by the availability of resources to purchase reliable and current information in a range of formats. Senior management will need to be persuaded of the importance of this. Chapter 7 considers some supporting information for careers education.

Facilitating young people's access to information can be problematic if those involved in IAP are not aware of the Action Planning Web (see Chapter 7) and thus the importance of partnerships between individuals and agencies. Without such knowledge young people may not be referred to others and thus may be deprived of opportunities to develop their knowledge and of possible sources of support which may assist them in undertaking their Action Plans.

Ownership and the Individual Action Plan

Just as empowerment necessitates a reconsideration of young people's roles in relation to their own learning, so does the principle that young people should own their Action Plan. Much emphasis is placed on the fact that the Action Plan is owned by the individual because it is about the young person and is created by him or her.

If the principle of ownership is accepted then there are a number of implications. If the Plan is the young person's, then additional copies of, or access to the IAP should be negotiated with the individual. Young people are unlikely during their education and training lives to have experienced similar requests. Young people need to understand what lies behind such negotiations, they should not be formulated in perfunctory ways in order to pass them off as unexceptional and to elicit the young person's ready agreement.

Institutions will need to think through the arguments readily advanced against young people literally owning their Plans. Some teaching staff claim Plans would be lost, or that the information is necessary for a range of other records and guidance activities. For some the main function of the Plan lies in its presentation to potential employers, trainers or educators at the point of transition. Aside from the questionable assumption that young people are bound to lose the IAP, the other concerns need to be considered on grounds of confidentiality. Teaching staff may be able to negotiate increased access to certain Action Plans by distinguishing between formative, confidential working Plans and those created for transition. If young people's Plans are to be prepared for a wider audience, they should be appraised of this before committing the outcomes of the IAP session to paper.

Individual ownership also raises questions about signing the document. Institutions should question what lies behind signing. Does the Plan belong to the young person and is it for their eyes only? Why should another sign a young person's individual Action Plan document? The reader is referred to questions about signing in Chapter 4.

Nothing Should be Placed on the Plan With Which the Individual Does Not Agree

Ownership and empowerment are allied closely to the principle that nothing should appear on the individual's Action Plan with which they do not agree. For anything to be placed on the Plan which does not reflect fully the young person, the planning session, and the issues discussed, is to invalidate the entire rationale behind Action Planning.

Teaching staff also need to be wary of writing on the Planning document for the young person. Adults may couch the import of the session too freely in their language rather than in that of the young person, thereby changing the young person's emphasis or meaning. Adults may misrepresent the session and the young person by prioritising their own concerns, by making value judgements, or censoring what the young person says. The adult partner may also inappropriately construct targets for the young person. The young person should be aware of their powers to veto an Action Plan with which they are unhappy. Again, they need to be made aware that they have such power and adults need to invite them to question what has been written.

It is important that what is on the Plan reflects the young person and the Planning session. It is important that what appears on the Plan can be read and understood by young people when they are alone. An incomprehensible plan, one written in too complex language or with small print, disempowers the young person and invalidates both the process and the Plan.

Individual Action Planning as an Ongoing Progress

Integral to the IAP process is the fact that it is a continuous process of taking stock, determining targets, undertaking and reviewing action, and planning accordingly. IAP is process based. It is not a one-off individual assessment. It is, at its most simple, a cycle of plan-do-review. Although it is useful for someone to undertake a counselling session to determine future action, the benefits of an ongoing process of structured action and review would be lost.

The ongoing nature of IAP means that it is a costly and labour-intensive process. However as the individual proceeds through structured IAP and review sessions with an experienced planning partner they will acquire and internalise some of the skills of self-review and self-analysis which will enable them to be more self-sufficient. Chapter 6 explores some other means of meeting the intense demands of Action Planning.

This brief chapter has looked at eight principles which underpin IAP. These principles have implications for any institution which decides to develop IAP. IAP makes demands on human and physical resources. It demands a flexible and responsive curriculum. IAP requires that teaching staff be responsive to students' needs and reconceptualise the ways they regard young people. The principles underlying IAP require that young people be accorded rights within the IAP session and the institution. IAP gives young people rights to control the flow of information and access to information which adults may try to gather about them.

The following chapter continues to explore some of the issues which surround the development and delivery of IAP.

6 Issues and Implications

Introduction

Chapter 5 began the process of exploring some of the broader issues involved in IAP. This chapter continues that process and addresses such questions as:

- Is IAP a mechanism of containment?
- Does IAP increase the educational pressures experienced by young people?
- Can IAP raise unrealisable expectations and what are the effects of this?
- How might Peer Planning assist in resourcing the IAP process?
- What may be problematic in parental involvement in their children's IAPs?

IAP – A Mechanism of Containment or Control?

Two educational sociologists, Hargreaves and Reynolds, have been concerned with recent educational policies which have led to decomprehensivisation, privatisation, market competitiveness, differentiation, centralisation and control. They have attacked a range of educational initiatives which create 'instruments of social surveillance' (Hargreaves and Reynolds, 1989, p.25).

Although IAP was in its infancy in 1989 when their book was published, its underlying principles could have been included in the list of 'pupil profiles, processes of self-assessment, negotiated assessment and recording of personal experiences' (Hargreaves and Reynolds, 1989, p.25).

Below, their observations on the pupil profiling movement are reproduced. These comments have direct application to IAP practices and have a justifiably provocative quality when IAP is considered in this light.

> 'Pupil profiles...were in danger of opening up pupils' emotions for hierarchical inspection, assessing personality as well as performance. They were designed to do this not just as a matter of entitlement, but of inescapable, enforced entitlement. And it appeared they would apply the process on a regular, routine basis where the pupil's knowledge of future inescapable

"negotiated" reviews would suppress deviance or non-conformity even before it arose. Profiles...might well lead to the build-up of sinister written or mental dossiers on pupils, which could be retrieved for possible use at later points in the child's educational career. They would subject emotion, feelings and intentions to mandatory scrutiny. And despite rhetorics of negotiation, this process of compulsory "review" would in most cases probably be predominantly one-sided, the teacher observing and judging the child, rather than vice versa.' (Hargreaves and Reynolds, 1989)

Some teaching staff engaged in early IAP development work have questioned whether Action Planning might be a means of controlling pupils (Squirrell,1992a). Certainly there are a number of ways in which this might occur. Teaching staff may try to impose their own targets on young people. They may try to force young people towards institutionally correct behaviours or inflict their own value judgements about beliefs and lifestyles. Teachers might collude with parents or other carers in creating targets which they feel more appropriate for young people. Any imposed targets may well run counter to the young person's own self-image and aims.

If young people do sign a Plan which contains imposed targets it is possible that teaching staff could use non-compliance during the review session as an additional means of castigating the young person. It is important that status of the document, as one which the young person controls, needs to be emphasised, as does the student's right of veto and free-will in adhering to or abandoning targets at any point while trying to action them.

Certainly the author of this text has witnessed some IAP sessions where a tutor's academic values and interests have dominated the session, overwhelming the student and finally becoming formalised as targets. Similarly the author's review of students' Action Plans in one institution revealed that young people at the close of year 12 were being heavily encouraged to adopt one of two pre-defined targets. This runs counter to the philosophy of IAP as a mechanism to identify and match individuals' needs, even though some may argue that judicious review of HE prospectuses or taking a driving test were useful goals.

Watts in his evaluation of the Essex County YDP had the following to say:

'...some young people perceive it as being "for them, not for me": this was reflected in a comment of one college student that the writing-down of plans was "for the lecturer to see what you're up to". Action planning could act as a control mechanism in two different respects:
– In terms of input, either influencing what is included ("You don't really want to do that, do you?") or determining it ("You must put that down..."). More subtly, such influence could operate through young people anticipating

what they think teachers and other adults want them to say.

– In terms of output, becoming a "stick to beat them with" – i.e. offering evidence which can be used against the young person. It could, for example, be a punitive tool for truculent pupils or reluctant learners, setting targets linked to sanctions and/or rewards. The report of the Essex County Inspectorate (1990) noted a tendency in two institutions for the action-planning process "to be used to chase recalcitrant students or to support weaker students".' (Watts,1992)

One further way in which IAP could be open to the charge of becoming an instrument of control lies in the decision making process which leads up to the selection of a choice of career or training route. Control may come about if teaching staff or parents have particularly clear visions of a young person and they may attempt to 'close down options'. Similarly if a young person has difficulty in reaching post-transition decisions, then the IAP may be used as a device to channel him or her away from prevarication or indecisiveness. This would be a misuse of IAP, all the more so if the IAP was later used as 'a stick with which to beat' the young person if he or she finally made a decision which better suited him or her.

Finally, if the completion of the Plan is allowed to become the sole objective for the IAP session then it may be possible that the tutor and student will be led away from discovery and only be concerned with sketching out containable and measurable goals.

Teaching staff advocating IAP development work and training colleagues, parents, employers and other end-users should be alive to the possibilities of any misuse of Action Plans. Where staff are made responsible for establishing IAP within an institution they should consider how they will monitor colleagues' implementation of Action Planning processes and documentation.

IAP Increasing the Pressures Experienced by Young People

There are a range of ways in which IAP might be experienced as a pressure by some young people. Some:

- may not wish to plan all the time;
- may find it difficult to formulate targets;
- may find having to reach their targets impossibly hard;
- may fear ridicule or exposure of their failure to reach targets;
- may not appreciate at the outset what their targets involve in terms of their commitment of time, energy or other resources. Thus completion of targets may become irksome and onerous.

Many of these possibilities can be forestalled by sensitive guidance. Young people need simple explanations about IAP and its potential role in their lives, this will help many to feel more in control. Tutors should re-iterate that the individual drives the planning process, determines the goals, their nature and number. The tutor should know when to 'back off', to leave target-setting alone, to stop probing about what was or was not achieved and why. The tutor should be able to assist the young person create success criteria and thus means by which the individual can measure progress.

The nature of the Action Plan and Planning Partner should be explained to the young person, it should be clearly explained that the document and the adult are to assist the student's development. The document and the role of the Planning Partner should not be endowed by either student or adult with any punitive qualities. The young person should not fear reprisals or recrimination for any failure to achieve a goal. The open discussion of targets abandoned or partially attempted should be as integral and valuable a part of IAP review sessions as discussions of completed goals. Young people should be encouraged to learn from all their experiences.

It may help tutors and students to undertake some post-target analysis. This was profitably undertaken by tutors, guidance workers and pupils of the St Austell YDP. A copy of the evaluation proforma they used is shown in Figure 6.1. Reviewing the cost and human resource implications of a target can help both adult planning partner and student evaluate

Figure 6.1 Post-Target Analysis

The target I set was:

What did I have to give up:

The help and support I had in achieving the target came from:

The problems I faced were:

I overcame these by doing the following:

The actual steps I needed to take to achieve this were:

The amount of time it took me to achieve the target was:

By achieving the target I have learned:

whether the result was worth the effort; how much effort he or she might wish to make next time and to gauge the likely demands of future goals. Such analysis will help the student and tutor determine what they may have overlooked in terms of potential problems or sources of help. It may help them to more effectively break subsequent targets into more easily realisable steps.

Finally, if thought is not given to the timing of IAP as it falls within students' educational life-cycle some can experience IAP as an additional pressure. One example is when the preparation of an IAP for transition into post-compulsory education, training or employment is conflated with exam revision and the concerns of facing adult life. This was experienced by some students as both taxing and terrifying (Squirrell,1991, 1992a). Tutors and IAP development workers need to consider when and how IAP is introduced to students and how much preparation for Action Planning is offered to students.

IAP and the Raising of Unrealisable Expectations

There are two ways in which IAP may inadvertently raise unreasonable expectations. Both of which can be prevented by quality guidance. Firstly and at a most basic level the young person should not leave the IAP session having set unreasonable targets. The targets may be unreasonable because they are too woolly, are simply unattainable or are too vast to be completed within the set timescale. The young person should be counselled away from expecting to achieve the impossible.

The tutor may be an accessory in setting unrealistic goals. Poor tutoring may lead the young person to accept goals to which they do not fully subscribe or may encourage the setting of too many goals. The following extract illustrates the latter.

> Tutor: 'Well I think we have agreed that you need to improve your attendance by next term, practise your handwriting and you are going to join the hockey club.'
> or
> Tutor: 'Which areas of our discussion on attendance, handwriting and outside interests do you feel you might like to work on?'

The latter is preferable, otherwise the tutor's requirements are being imposed on the student.

The young person's expectations may unrealistically be raised if the individual is permitted to leave the session having set a goal which is absurd because his or her current levels of achievement may suggest it unlikely, or because the goals runs counter to a professed lifestyle preference, commitment or to physical abilities, or finally because specific employment goals may not be realisable in particular local or national labour markets.

IAP does not serve the individual well if such outcomes are allowed. The tutor should be skilled enough to confront unrealistic expectations. The tutor should not denigrate either the ambition nor the individual but should assist the young person to such self-appreciation that the goal may be modified or changed and the reasons for so doing, understood.

Comprehensive counselling, reference to sources of expert careers advice and guidance on training courses should accompany Action Planning at transition. Where this does not happen the IAP sessions will not meet young people's legitimate needs and some will set their occupational sights on goals for which they may be ill-suited or which they poorly comprehend. Young people should be appraised of the demands and the nature of occupation they favour and any training required for entry.

Resourcing IAP and the Potential of Peer Planning

One of the most trenchant criticisms of IAP is that it is labour intensive. This cannot be disputed. The value of IAP comes from the time spent in attentive one to one interaction. The importance of taking stock, of reviewing progress, of encouraging, and helping to critically examine issues and action, cannot be undertaken in any way other than through working alongside another person.

Most frequently the Planning Partner is an adult. However young people can be effective additional Planning Partners. Peer Planning has been tried with young people across the range of school and college ages and has been found to work successfully.

Peer Planning is not a substitute for the professional input of a trained adult. It cannot replace the knowledge of expert adults or the benefits from appropriate referral or counselling. However, Peer Planning has enormous merit in supplementing the limited human resources of adult members of staff, it allows for more regular and even quite spontaneous review sessions. Peer Planning may also enable some chary of talking to adults or uncertain about particular issues to be more forthcoming.

Young people need to be trained in Peer Planning. There are the anticipatable problems of competition or over-critical comments. Young people need to be offered ground rules and the reasoning behind them. Basic counselling principles of listening, non-directive comments and trying to summarise are useful skills for Peer Planners to learn. Similarly an appreciation of the mutuality of working with another and the swapping of roles is important to foster. A rehearsal of principles such as listening, non-critical comment and confidentiality should be explored in order to create some climate of trust.

A further strategy for supplementing adult resources has been that of group planning. Working in groups may perhaps preclude the discussion of each individual's Plan. However it teaches a range of important interative and group based skills. Such skills include: active listening, considering appropriate contributions, encouraging others, exploring each other's concerns, learning to work as a member of a team, appreciating others' achievements, exploring one's own potential with others, evaluating what others say about oneself, learning when to ask for help, advice or support and developing self-help strategies with peers.

Group planning also allows peers to share others' concerns and interests. Sometimes hearing about other people's targets and progress can encourage young people to value what they have achieved or to broaden their own ideas of what may be possible for them.

There have been instances where group planning and review sessions have led to collective Action Plans. This can arise when young people have been sharing problems with particular subjects or aspects of learning. Collective agreements have led to discussions of their concerns with appropriate teachers and support groups to sustain one another through particularly difficult pieces of work.

Another example of a collective action strategy occurred amongst a group of trainees. The employment area for which they were training was suddenly devastated by the effects of the recession. They worked together to sustain each other's motivation and commitment in the absence of the carrot of employment. They also worked collectively to think around the problems in seeking employment.

The adult facilitating a planning group will need to rehearse some ground-rules, help create an atmosphere of confidence and trust, and confront displays of competition, inattentiveness, and overly critical or destructive comment.

The Potentially Problematic Parental Influence

Parents' roles are potentially problematic but they are an important element in the success or otherwise of a young person's IAP experience. Parents may exert their influence and potential support for the benefit of young people or to their detriment.

Parents can be unhelpful to young people when they are able to work against the ethos of the IAP as a process and product which is owned by the young person. Where parents are able to set goals or to undermine the young person's targets, the student may lose motivation or interest. This is especially so where students are very young and dependent upon parents for financial resources, for physical help such as lifts to clubs or courses or for additional motivation, support and encouragement to persist with a goal.

Parents' wishes and significance cannot be underestimated especially when young people are at the point of transition into post-16 education, training or employment. Teaching staff will have to consider how they may deal with a situation where students' and parents' expectations clash.

Tutoring staff will need to take some time to consider the role of parents and their own strategies for explaining IAP work to parents and enlisting their help. Teaching staff will need to be aware that some parents will be critical of what they perceive to be interference in or additional pressure on their children's lives.

Two final issues, both highly germane to the quality of the IAP process and to young people's experience of it are confidentiality and evaluation. These are considered in Chapter 7 which addresses issues of institutional development and management of IAP.

This chapter has considered five issues in the delivery of IAP. Three of these issues were discussed as possibilities if the processes of guidance and tutoring were lacking. Thus IAP was explored as a possible device for increasing students' experiences of stress and pressure, for encouraging or fostering unreasonable expectations and the corollary of experiencing failure and finally, the possibility that IAP might be a means to control or contain young people. The burden was laid on the shoulders of those responsible for developing IAP to ensure that tutors were trained to confront and not foster unrealistic expectations and to ensure relevant referrals. IAP development teams were charged with monitoring the processes, the use of Action Plans in the sessions and to consider how young people might be approaching and experiencing their targets.

Tutors had a continuing role for they had to assist the development of peer and group planning if it was to be effective and not to flounder in possible counter-productive competitiveness. It was suggested that peers could be of great help in offering another experience of IAP to their colleagues. It was a supplement to the IAP which would be undertaken with an adult, but would nevertheless develop transferable skills and at its best offer a quality of supportiveness which no adult planning partner would be able to extend or perhaps sustain.

The final issue was that of the parental role. It is an area which staff embarking upon IAP will have to consider. It is one where there are a number of potential pitfalls and areas of conflict if students' and parental wishes fail to coincide. Tutoring staff could find that they are unfortunately trapped between charges of abandoning their students after talking of empowerment and being seen by parents to interfere in their children's lives.

These issues require consideration by staff embarking on IAP and merit time in the initial and on going in-service work on IAP. The next chapter considers the management of IAP at the broader institutional level and these five potentially problematic areas are likely to feature in any in-house discussions by institutions embarking upon IAP. These issues over-lap with others such as confidentiality, the systemic implications of such issues as it addresses the processes of the institutional development and management of IAP.

7 Developing and Managing Individual Action Planning

Introduction

As with the IAP cycle itself there are a number of clear stages which need to be worked through in order to initiate, develop and establish IAP within an institution and to ensure that effective partnerships are created with agencies and individuals beyond the institution. This chapter focuses on the practical steps in developing IAP within an educational institution.

There are several stages in establishing IAP practices within a school or college. Some involve tasks such as evaluation, which are on-going, while others, for example building an effective IAP development team, are concentrated at the outset of the work. For the purposes of this chapter, four stages and their associated tasks are considered. These are:

- starting out;
- early implementation;
- consolidation and extension;
- creating partnerships beyond the institution.

The accounts of these stages are not exhaustive, but the chapter should offer a reasonable check-list for developing IAP at an institutional level.

Stage 1: Starting Out

In thinking about beginning IAP within your institution a number of preparatory tasks have to be undertaken. As with any educational initiative there is little to be gained from being a lone or hero innovator. From the outset it is important to have the support of senior managers and to have a team of committed colleagues.

The Roles of Senior Managers

Senior managers are vital to the success of any initiative, having an overview of the institution and its development. They initiate policy and contribute to an ethos congenial to developing Individual Action Planning. Managers can, by freeing time for the training of all staff or placing IAP on the institutional development plan, signify its importance and their commitment to it.

Senior managers can also ensure that those responsible for compatible areas of development work can complement each another. Managers can designate time for staff discussion, the sharing of development ideas and in-service training.

Senior managers can ensure that an effective development team is created. Such a team should represent a broad range of institutional interests and be composed of staff who command respect.

Senior mangers as policy-makers and controllers of resources are enormously influential on the success or failure of any initiative.

Senior managers and policy-making

The IAP development team will need to refer to senior managers for guidance in developing IAP principles and proposed practice. Such areas might include the confidentiality of IAP sessions and documentation; the production, quality and storage of Plans; the ownership of and access to Action Plans; and the use of information technology and young people's access to it. Senior managers will need to contribute to decision-making about the focus, extent and forms of monitoring. Management will need to explore with the development team how the monitoring process would be resourced and undertaken, and how the outcomes might be used.

Policy-makers will need to consider issues of equality of opportunity and the means for its evaluation. Equal opportunities policies should be broad enough to cover young people with differing levels of current educational achievement, diverse educational or training needs and with various longer-term learning aspirations. Such policies should recognise that young people from different social backgrounds have unequal access to social and economic opportunities, and that they may have differing levels of self-confidence, self-esteem, and differing degrees of self-advocacy and self-management.

Such policies need to address race and gender. Teaching staff and pupils will need to know what recourse they have should they feel unfairly or prejudicially treated or harassed during the IAP sessions. They will need to know what might be expected of the IAP sessions and what their roles and those of others would entail.

Senior management and resourcing

As the administrators of institutional resources, managers control the time and funding for staff training and the ways the timetable could be organised to foster an initiative, for example in creating time for one-to-one interviews with students. Such control extends to designating the space available for interview areas, and how the careers library, its staffing and stock might be developed. Managers' control of resources will also affect the type and quality of IAP documentation, and whether and how information technology is used.

Senior managers' will also be the ones to set aside resources for monitoring or evaluation, and for training staff in monitoring practices. Staff involved in monitoring will need time for the collection and analysis of data, for its dissemination and for planning how findings might inform future practices. Funding may also be needed for the production of evaluation proformas.

Senior managers' continued support will be necessary to maintain the position of IAP and to allocate the time it will take in the face of other developmental initiatives and statutory demands. Management's continued commitment will also be necessary if learning provision and styles of teaching and learning are to be responsive to students' identified learning needs.

The IAP Development Team

Composition of the development team

Individual teachers or tutors who institute IAP will need to create a broad-based team to initiate the work and to take early decisions on its implementation and possible development. The team would ideally consist of staff with experience in developmental work, and with a range of interests and complementary curriculum and assessment skills. It would be preferable if some members of the development team were experienced teachers and had status within the institution. This would endow the team's work with kudos and may facilitate communication with senior management.

A broad-based development team brings together experience and understanding of many areas of the curriculum. This creates a firm base for an early curriculum audit. Such a team will be able to make a number of overtures to a wide range of staff by talking about IAP, determining their early responses to it and their training needs in order to implement it. This may help increase initial acceptance of the IAP work. A broad based development team may mean that it has a greater range of expertise to draw upon for early in-house training.

From the outset the team will have to address a number of questions. Some answers may be determined by pragmatic concerns, such as the areas of the curriculum where IAP would most easily rest or the type of staff who are willing to be involved in IAP. Managerial decisions may also determine early development work. Such as which students should be involved, whether IAP should be started with one year group, with a particular tutor or subject group, or whether it should be initiated across the whole school or college.

The development and management teams will need to address such questions as those listed below.

Taking early decisions

Consider the following in the context of your institution:

What is understood by IAP?

Why does the institution want to embark on IAP?
How would IAP benefit young people in your institution?
How will Action Plans be used and by whom?
How are IAP principles such as ownership and
empowerment understood within the context of your
institution?
To what extent can they be endorsed?
Who would have access to information from IAP sessions or held on
Action Plans? Why would they have access to information?
Which young people would be targeted for IAP and why?
How many might be involved initially?
Would there be a pilot group in one or two year groups or would IAP
be started with a whole year group?
How would IAP be integrated with other current school
or college activities such as work experience or the production of
personal statements?

Would IAP be given separate timetabled time or would it be part of
tutorial or other activities?
Which staff would undertake IAP?
Would staff or young people be able to contract out?
Would only interested staff be approached, or only
those involved with a particular year group or in a
particular curriculum area?
Would staff and young people be matched or would
pairings for IAP sessions be on the basis of free
choice?
How would this process of pairing be managed?
How frequently would IAP take place and at whose
instigation?

Rationalising documentation

The core team and senior managemers will need to consider the relationships between IAP documentation, their own RoA, the NRA and between

IAPs and the Action Plans created for Training Credits and those which are part of the Careers Service Summaries of Guidance. Such early decisions are important, for where teachers and learners perceive unnecessary overlaps in documentation they are less likely to endorse and engage with Action Planning. As IAP documentation is perhaps of less significance than the process, it would seem foolhardy to jeopardize commitment to the process through repetitious collection of information and completion of similar documentation. Such a review of documentation and relationships at this stage will clarify institutional understanding of the roles of various in-house colleagues and partners in the Careers Guidance Service.

An early curriculum review

During this period of determining the foundations for future development work, a curriculum audit should be undertaken. The development team should determine where practices such as target setting, creating success criteria, monitoring progress, review and experientially informed planning are already taking place within the institution. The audit may also reveal natural links between the proposed IAP work and work experience, careers education, flexible learning, RoA, GNVQ, Core Skills work, personal development work in PSE, and the transition arrangements for students. Where the development team can identify similar activities or demonstrate the complementary quality of IAP to other work, then colleagues may become more convinced of the feasibility of undertaking IAP and of their own capacity for so doing.

During this period of setting up, decisions will have been made about the foundations for implementation. some areas of policy, and information will have been gathered from a curriculum review. This early period will also involve data collection about the availability and type of resources, and staff training needs.

Planning early training

Staff and students will need to be skilled in the IAP process and in using Action Plans. Some training, for example in using Action Plans at transition, could be undertaken later, but from the outset young people and staff need to be appraised of the rationale behind IAP and of its potential benefits.

The team would have to research what materials were already available in school or college to assist the training process, and what needed to be devised or could be purchased. The team would need to determine what skills were available in-house and who beyond the school or college could be approached to undertake training. At this stage the Careers Service or TEC personnel may be useful sources of help.

Early training and information would need to be IAP-specific, for example dealing with the IAP process, the roles of the Planning Partner and the learner, the rationale behind IAP, potential benefits from IAP and the possible uses of Action Plans. More generalised training and information sessions are needed in areas pertinent to all formative assessment practices, for example in raising self-awareness, in developing listening and questioning skills, in determining success criteria, and in the collection of evidence and reviewing achievement.

During early training the significance and the role of evaluation should also be discussed. Such discussions should cover how the process and product may be evaluated, how data might be collected and used. At this stage fears about evaluation leading to scrutiny or appraisal of teaching staff may need to be explored.

Following this stage of early decision-making, team building and giving thought to issues about procedures and documentation, then the next stage of implementation can begin.

Stage 11: The Early Implementation of IAP

There are three main tasks in this phase. These are training staff and pupils, early delivery of IAP sessions and the creation of Action Plans, and evaluation. These tasks are discussed below.

Informing and Training Staff and Students

Informing staff

Following early decision-making, certain staff and students will have been targetted for IAP. Although only certain staff may immediately be involved in IAP sessions and in creating Action Plans, all staff should be informed that IAP is taking place in their institution. They should be appraised of the ways in which IAP links with the whole curriculum and pre-existing assessment practices. Aside from tactical gains from informing staff early on, it will also alert staff to IAP practices, arouse interest, and make some aware that students may approach them for help, information or advice. It should be emphasised at this point that staff disinterest, lack of understanding and failure to support students during the early stages of delivery could undermine learners' efforts.

The IAP development team should be as clear in their expectations of the broad staff group as they are of those staff who are targeted for early and full involvement in IAP. There are any number of ways to brief the staff group: flyers, information leaflets, brief presentations and question and answer sessions. The team should be able to describe the processes of IAP, its rationale and potential benefits, they should be able to outline their plans for supporting staff and able to field colleagues' objections.

Typically, staff may voice concerns about IAP leading to further changes in their teaching or tutoring roles, imposing more demands upon them and necessitating the acquisition of more skills. Some teaching staff may feel ill-equipped to work alongside young people in the role of a Planning Partner or may feel uncomfortable in a counselling role. Many staff will express concern that IAP will put pressure on existing resources. IAP may be perceived as 'yet another initiative' or as an activity already done elsewhere within the curriculum or through Careers Guidance Services. IAP may therefore be seen as unnecessary duplication or as an ephemeral educational activity. Many of these concerns or objections can be met. Staff need to be informed of the training and resourcing to be provided, and of the ways in which IAP can be accommodated in the timetable. Staff should be told of the importance of IAP in yielding immediate benefits to young people, the institution and teaching staff, and that over the longer term young people will acquire transferable skills. The centrality of IAP to a range of assessment, guidance and training activities within and beyond school and college should be explained. Staff concern that IAP might prove repetitious can be countered with discussion about the value of reinforcing such skills as planning, target setting, review and self-evaluation. Staff should also be made aware of the value for young people in acquiring IAP skills early in their educational careers and of the beneficial cumulative effect of practising IAP processes. Concerns about repetition and needless duplication are important ones and can also be tackled by inviting discussion about current curriculum and assessment procedures in an attempt to rationalise in the longer term what students are offered. Some other concerns which staff might raise have been detailed in Chapter 6, to which the reader is referred.

Training staff

For those staff more immediately engaged in IAP processes and in producing documentation with young people, specific training will be needed in addition to the more general information offered to the whole staff group. The following may need to be addressed:

- general formative assessment processes and the links between such processes and IAP;

- counselling skills;
- the detailed processes and the principles of IAP;
- the roles of the Planning Partner and the learner;
- the rules and boundaries for IAP sessions;
- the role of IAP within and beyond the institution; a focus on integration and partnership;
- what IAP means within and to the institution.

Much of the material needed for information and training sessions can be extrapolated from the earlier chapters of this book. In addition the development team should discover what the local TEC and LEA may be providing to support IAP work.

Staff training may begin by brainstorming to elicit what is already understood about IAP and what they perceive their roles and those of the students to be, and to explore why they think the institution has become involved. Such brainstorming may be prompted by questions such as:

- What do you understand by Individual Action Planning?
- Why is Individual Action Planning done?
- How is Individual Action Planning done?
- How would IAP fit in with current practices in the school/college?
- What demands might IAP make on the school/college?
- What do you expect your role to be?
- What is the role of young people?
- Who could help you in your role?
- What information or training might you need?
- What are your concerns about being involved in IAP?

From these general questions discussion may lead to considering:

- the importance of process before product;
- the benefits from IAP to the individual, to staff and for the institution;
- the roles in the immediate IAP partnership;
- the availability of support: the IAP development team, partners in the Careers Service, the input of senior managers, and longer-term partnerships with parents and employers.

From practical concerns and considerations the discourse may move to a discussion of the principles of IAP, and to the more problematic areas of ownership, empowerment and quality assurance. These issues can be explored initially in the abstract and then how they might fit with the institution.

One aspect of IAP which predictably will generate staff concern is that of undertaking a counselling role with young people. Some guidance points for counselling were offered in Chapter 2. The following material may be useful for staff training and discussion focused on counselling skills and conducting an IAP session.

The materials include:

- a checklist for managing an IAP session;
- an overview of the stages of the IAP discourse;
- fragment of a formative assessment interview.

A CHECKLIST FOR MANAGING AN IAP SESSION

Having arranged an appointment with the student:

1 PREPARATION Review any previous information collected from the student and determine any follow up points to be included in the discussion. Sort the IAP agenda. Collect any relevant information.

2 ORGANISATION Arrange for a quiet room and take steps to prevent interruptions, e.g. cancel phone calls or leave a sign on the office door.

3 OPENING Be clear about the purpose of the interview, encourage the student to comment and to add other issues.

4 CONDUCTING THE SESSION Give your full attention throughout. Discuss confidentiality with the student. Ensure that the student knows that it is his or her time. Be clear how much time is available. Be aware of your own agenda. Make clear the stages of the interview. Decide who writes notes, whether an IAP form is filled out and why. Encourage comments. Above all listen to the student. Summarise and explore what the student has said. Help the student formulate targets, check that he or she understands the action which is to be undertaken, outline clearly mutual responsibilities and who else may be asked for help.

5 CONTINUITY Set a date, approximate or otherwise, for a review session. Be guided by student needs.

OVERVIEW OF THE STAGES OF AN IAP SESSION

INTRODUCTION

Ensure that the student is welcomed, feels comfortable and has under-taken any necessary preparatory work.

NEGOTIATION

Check that the student understands the aims and purpose of the inter-view and agrees to them. Enable the student to add their concerns and areas for discussion.

EXPLORATION AND DEVELOPMENT OF THE YOUNG PERSON AND THEIR IDEAS

This includes:

– information gathering about the student's interests, qualities achievements, concerns.

– encouraging self-assessment by the student. Feed back statements to encourage greater clarification and the exploration of inconsisten-cies.

– encouraging the young person to discuss a range of ideas, options and alternatives. Tease out concerns, suitability and feasibility.

– identifying information needs, giving information which is asked for and where it is possible to do so. Make referrals. Summarise dis-cussion. Note possible alternative actions and options.

SETTING TARGETS

Determine with the young person the most realistic options. Encour-age the young person to fashion targets. Ensure the young person wants to be committed to those targets and help them determine ways to measure success and to make their targets time-bound. Emphasise that not to achieve targets does not mean failure. Encourage the young person to think about and record why they may have abandoned a tar-get. Determine with the student a date for review of progress and possible reconsideration of the Plan.

Effective listening and questioning skills are hard to cultivate. Teaching staff may need to be guided through some of the techniques and encour-aged to evaluate their mastery and use of such skills. The following is an extract from some research on pupil–teacher negotiation by Hilary Rad-nor (1992). The excerpt offers what a teacher considers to be formative assessment, the outcome of which is the completion of a statement:

> *I.T*: ...I've got to write down about your attainment, your effort and your attendance, but we'll come onto that later. Your attainment and effort are excellent. You work very well, I think – and this is what I'd like to put down

here. You work well, you're full of enthusiasm – you didn't know I was going to tell you all this, did you?

2.P: No.

3.T: You're keen, you've got excellent ideas, great imaginative ideas that you put into practice and that you contribute well to others.

4.P: Thanks.

5.T: All right? And that's what I'd like to put. You've also finished your piece of coursework that I set you on the production. So I want to put that as well. You're up to date with your coursework. Now let me phrase this. [T reads aloud as he is writing.]

"Simon works with an excellent attitude. He is full of enthusiasm and is talented in this subject." Now, I've got to look back throughout the year and I've got to say this has shown in every lesson – which it has, really – throughout this year since last September.

6.P: Yeah. I think our whole group together work really well.

7.T: They do, don't they?

8.P: Yeah.

9.T: [Writes down what he has just said] "This has shown in every lesson since last September." Splendid. I can't really put "I look forward to seeing your 5th year work" because this is a summary so far but I am looking forward to seeing your 5th year work. I think your ideas are mature, really, for 15 – for 4th year going on 5th year. I think you've got some... I want to put something about that as well. [Looks to pupil for consent.]

10.P: Yeah, sure yeah. I think we all put our ideas in together so it works out, really, because we all, like, contribute.

11.T: Fine. So, after you say that, you'd like me to put something about the group as well, would you?

12.P: Yeah, say "he works well with the whole group". Just put he has good ideas and works well as a whole with the rest of the group.

13.T: Yes. [Writing.] "The group works so well as a whole unit."

14.P: And Simon contributes with ideas or ...

15.T: Yes, you do. That's fine.

Radnor (1992) offers the following commentary:

The quality of this discourse was teacher control 1,3, and pupil response 2,4. The teacher generated the statements, provided the value judgements and articulated the achievement leaving the pupil to either agree or disagree. The expectation of the pupil to have an agenda other than the teacher's was not even an issue. Teacher and pupil responded to each other's expectations, teacher controls the pacing and structure of both the interview and the content of the interview, the pupil complies. This is an example of the kind of profiling discourse between teacher and pupil where the teacher is not behaving in a collaborative way with the pupil which the term "negotiation" implies. It is assessing the pupil, measuring his achievements.'

Questioning, guiding and listening skills are ones which many teaching staff will need to cultivate. Some pointers to effective questioning and listening follow below.

Questioning

The student and tutor need to determine common understanding of the young person in order to undertake any future planning. Questioning is a means of establishing common ground. The IAP session should, however, not become a time of intense scrutiny nor one of staccato questioning which leaves the student perplexed and uncomfortable. The tutor should explain what question areas lie ahead and why such questions are being asked. The student should be asked to comment on the question areas, asked to offer others if he or she desires, and be made aware that he or she does not have to answer. The student should throughout the session know that he or she is in control of what is asked and answered. Questioning should not:

1 *Lead* – dictate to the student that there is only one answer to a question and that is the one which the tutor suggests.
2 *Block or close* – ignore the student's agenda and close down or belittle his or her concerns.
3 *Dispute* – assert that what the student says is not valid or important.

Questioning should enable the tutor and student to have a clearer understanding. Thus questioning should:

1 *Clarify* – Check that the tutor or the student has understood an issue and has shared understanding.
2 *Encourage* – Enable the student to continue with, expand upon or explore an issue. The young person should feel able to do so however tentatively.
3 *Summarise* – Draw together the key themes and issues.
4 *Reinforce* – Support the students' understandings, perceptions, the main concerns once they have been explored.
5 *Focus* – Help the young person determine what are the key concerns and aims and the strategies for dealing with or meeting them (North Yorkshire Youth Development Project, 1992a).

Alongside the development of questioning skills tutors will need to cultivate their powers of active listening.

Listening

Many teaching staff have commented that teaching and listening are almost incompatible. As one teacher phrased it, 'listening is beaten out of us' (Squirrell, 1992a). A crucial element in establishing a quality IAP relationship is the planning partner being an active listener.

Developing active listening skills will include:

- Awareness of appropriate body language and appropriate use of eyes.
- Making use of minimal statements or interjections which demonstrate attentiveness and support but which do not intrude, for example, 'is that so', 'tell me more', 'yes?', 'umm', 'good– so you mean?'
- Reiteration of some of the main ideas or concerns can make the young person appreciate he/she is being listened to and that he or she should go on.

The tutor should not be afraid of silence: it can help both tutor and student collect their thoughts.

Paraphrasing and asking for clarification are also helpful, but there is no point in deliberately trying to misinterpret what has been said. If there are discrepancies these should be approached openly but not in such a way to confuse or corner the young person. Degrees of ambiguity and conflicting wishes are, after all, quite human.

The tenor of the IAP session should be to explore, to allow tentativeness and trialling of ideas. The tutors' questioning and listening strategies should encourage this. The tutor should ask him or herself at the close of each interview if he or she did all that was possible to create an environment which enabled the student to explore what he or she wanted. The tutor should also scrutinise his or her own listening or questioning strategies to determine how much of the young person's narrative was closed down, cut across or still remained at the close of the session unclear. Tutor self-evaluation should be encouraged by the development team. Tutors might perhaps be provided with a brief proforma to consider and complete. However, such monitoring devices should have outcomes and should not be allowed to dominate the proceedings.

Informing and Training Young People

Throughout this discussion of IAP emphasis has been placed on empowering the individual learner to take control over the process and outcomes of IAP. The induction of young people into IAP has to be underpinned by this.

This may of course mean that the induction proceeds less than smoothly. Students may challenge teaching staff as to why they are having to Action Plan. The importance of empowerment means that induction sessions have to be prepared thoroughly: students will need the rationale, process and outcomes of IAP clearly explained. Students will need to know about their role and what may be expected of them. They will need to be told about the roles which could be played by others, for example subject teachers or tutors, the planning partner, parents, employers, the Careers Service and later on by staff in those establishments to which they transfer.

The process of preparing detailed student briefings will demand that teachers reconsider their roles and attitudes towards students, for the latter will have to be treated as entitled to information and as responsible for driving and determining some aspects of their own learning.

Young people need to be fully informed about IAP in order to determine how and whether they will participate, so they will be able to understand what they may risk by minimal co-operation. Young people, like some teaching staff, may raise concerns about and objections to becoming involved in IAP. Initiators of IAP need to remember that young people, like teaching staff, will have experienced many changes in their school and college careers and may not be predisposed to undertake yet another initiative. Young people may advance specific objections, for example:

- that life is serendipity and they do not wish to plan;
- that there is no need to plan if they already have viable careers ideas;
- that planning and target setting create pressures;
- that by planning their career options may be closed down;
- that the IAP documents may be open to scrutiny;
- that the IAP sessions may be intrusive.

Young people may also object on grounds that IAP seems to repeat aspects of work undertaken in PSE, RoA and Careers Education. Young people may express concerns that IAP could create add to their workload. Some already determined on a course of action or who do not want to engage in self-reflection may argue that for them IAP is a pointless and time-wasting activity.

Teaching staff should be able to discuss such concerns. From the outset, however, teaching staff should be aware that young people may not want to plan all the time and that target setting can be perceived as onerous. Teaching staff should try to market IAP as helping young people acquire a set of transferable life-skills, as an activity which can help them take control of aspects of their own lives, and as something which need not always involve academic work or remedying weaknesses. IAP should be described as something which can enhance leisure time, foster personal development and help young people to realise personal ambitions. It should be made clear that target setting is a flexible activity and one which does not have to be a feature of every IAP or review session.

Young people may not immediately absorb all the nuances of difficult and unfamiliar concepts, such as the internalisation of the locus of control, empowerment and ownership, and taking responsibility for themselves. Young people may have difficulties with target setting, determining success criteria, collecting evidence, and personally monitoring and evaluating progress. These are not easy activities nor ones integral to all aspects of young people's educational careers. The explication of the process, rationale and potential gains from IAP may well require several repetitions.

Students will themselves become more sophisticated in their interrogation of the process, its applications and the role of documentation as they become more experienced planners. Their comments, insights, decisions about what is of value to them and suggestions for improvement could and, if the principles of ownership, empowerment and student-centredness are adhered to, should be sought and incorporated into the institution's plans for the future.

In addition to informing young people about IAP, there should be a training programme to equip them with the skills needed to engage successfully with the IAP process, to acquire transferable skills and to use IAP documentation. Again, the reader is referred to Chapters 2–4 for discussion of these skills involved and some suggestions for developing them. There are further references in the bibliography to materials which can be used with young people.

Evaluating early delivery of IAP processes and creation of Action Plans

It is important that early IAP sessions are monitored. Data is needed on the students' and teachers' perceptions of what has taken place, and their views on the value of such sessions, their longer-term utility and on any written documentation which was produced.

Early monitoring will reveal perceptions, areas where information is needed, misinformation and inconsistencies in practices. It will also reveal the range of interpretations of IAP. It is likely that staff involved as primary planning partners will have modified the process or the Plan as they internalise and take ownership of IAP.

Early evaluation will also demonstrate the effects of taking different approaches to IAP, for example, between pre-structured IAP questions and prompts and more free-flowing IAP sessions.

Those staff involved in the analysis of evaluation data will need to be alive to the fact that it will probably be a novel experience for many teaching staff and students. Thus a number of training needs and points for further information might be highlighted. The novelty may also give rise to criticism of IAP, and to accounts of young people or staff feeling uncomfortable or questioning the value of the exercise. It is possible that many negative feelings or perceptions may be born from the teachers' or students' unfamiliarity with IAP and may evaporate with protracted exposure to the process. Data should therefore be collected over several IAP sessions to determine if habit and understanding ease criticism and any sense of discomfort.

However, clearly identified training needs, areas for further information, or commonly held misinterpretations or misunderstandings should be acted upon. Pilot work has revealed the significance of careful and clear explanation to students. Where this has not taken place, whole groups of young people can pass through a process with no understanding of what they are doing and thus harbour concerns about the waste of their time. Early evaluation can also alert the development team to practices which if allowed to develop will undermine IAP as an educative and empowering process for young people. Areas in which it may be useful to collect data may include the extent to which the young person felt listened to, the extent to which they experienced a sense of pressure, for example in setting themselves targets or accepting the planning partners' targets. Should negative data emerge the development team would have to intervene. Early evaluation might include some of the following questions and question areas.

EARLY EVALUATION QUESTIONS FOR YOUNG PEOPLE

Biographical details of the learner and number of IAP/Review ses-sions attended.

Entry
How and when was IAP explained to you?
What did you think that it would offer you? Has it lived up to this?
What do you understand IAP to be about?

Content of IAP
Are the questions which you have been asked covered areas which you find it useful to discuss?
What else do you think should be included in the discussion to make it more useful to you?
Are there any types of question you find difficult or embarrassing to answer?

Conduct of IAP Session
It is helpful to you to talk to someone else about yourself and your future?
Do you find this easy to do? (Why? – adult? outsider?)
Do you find it easy to talk to strangers/adults anyway?
Do you feel that you are listened to?
Are there any ways in which your IAP sessions could be improved (longer/shorter/more frequent/at a different time of year)?
Do you think about your IAP/Review sessions before you have them?

Targets
Thinking back to the targets which were set:
Did you set them yourself?
Did you feel any pressure to set targets?
Was there enough time to complete them?
Can you talk about some of the targets you completed? What helped you to complete them?
Were there any you did not complete of that you changed? What were they? Why did you not complete/change them?
Do you set targets for yourself outside IAP sessions? – Why/why not?
Is target setting useful to you? Why/why not?

The IAP document
Has it been to useful to you to have your IAP written out?
Have you referred to it? When?
For what reasons?
How do you think it might be useful in the future? Would you know how to use it, e.g. job or training interviews?

Overview
Thinking about the IAP process as a whole:
Does the IAP fit into anything else that you are doing e.g. tutorial time, Careers Education, Record of Achievement, at a club or other out-of-school activity?
Has it helped you in any way?
Are you the type of person who thinks aobut yourself/your future any-way?
Has IAP helped you to discover anything about yourself?
Do your talk about your IAP or show it to anyone else? Who did you choose and why? What was their response?
Overall is there anything which could be done to make IAP better?

EARLY EVALUATION QUESTIONS FOR TEACHING/TUTORING STAFF

What do you understand IAP to be about?
What did you think IAP would offer you and the students you are working with?
Is it living up to your expectations?

Contents

Do the IAP sessions seem to cover useful areas? What might be missing?
Do you ask students to add their own concerns?
What else should be included in the discussion?
Are there any types of question you find difficult to ask or pupils find hard to answer?
What are students gaining from these sessions in the short and longer term (give examples).
What are the strengths and weaknesses of the IAP process?
Identify any areas where you feel you need further training to deal with IAP.
Whast support other than training do you need?
How is IAP linking with other school/college-based activities?
How adequate is the time made available for the IAP sessions?
Is more time needed? For what? Why?
How might existing time be used more effectively?
Have Action Plans been completed?
Are they being used? Is so, how?
How could the document be improved?
Do young people need training in using the documents?

If the decision was made early on that data collected through written pro-formas or interview would be fed into future development work, then an analysis of the information gathered from the types of question areas outlined above may be used to refine the process, to determine future training needs and in designing documentation.

As young people become more used to the process they could be asked to design IAP documents and to write user guides to the IAP process and Plans. Such work would give insights into what they found valuable and would enable effective targeting of information in language which young people understood. There is an example of a guide produced by young people in the Appendix.

Stage I I I: Consolidation and Expansion

Following evaluation of the early trialling of training materials, training sessions, delivery of IAP and creation of Plans, there will be much information to use to develop subsequent induction and support material and possibly to modify the way IAP is approached and documents produced. Once this next stage of development work is underway, it too needs to be evaluated.

The period of consolidation and extension should be marked by a number of tasks, such as:

- extending access to IAP to more learners;
- integrating IAP processes and outcomes across the range of school and college activities;
- developing the information base necessary to sustain IAP;
- working in partnership with other agencies and, of course,
- continued evaluation.

Extending access to IAP and increasing its integration

Once trialling and evaluation have suggested that quality IAP processes and documentation are attainable, the development team in conjunction with senior managers can decide how IAP is to be extended to other students. This may be done as an extension of the way in which IAP started, for example as a year 10 group becomes year 11, a second year 10 group can be initiated into IAP and the staff in contact with both years 10 and 11 can be involved. IAP can be expanded from one subject area to another. Extension may be more *ad hoc*, as teaching staff voice interest and volunteer to work with groups of students.

As more staff and young people become involved, the whole staff group will need to be made aware of the ways IAP is developing. Ideally as IAP extends within the institution more staff should be trained and encouraged to use IAP. Even the partial adoption of IAP practices across other subject areas, informing teaching and learning styles and assessment practices will reinforce young people's use and understanding of IAP. This will further the integration of IAP into the whole institution and support the increasing numbers of students using IAP to manage their learning.

It would be appropriate at this point, if it has not already taken place, for there to be the formal integration of experiential planning and target setting within the review processes and records maintained by all teaching staff.

Developing the information base to support IAP

At the heart of IAP is the assertion that it will assist young people to make informed decisions. The breadth of the IAP process and the age of the young people involved will dictate what information they may need. It may include uses of leisure time, ways to assist the development of personal and social competences, study skills, information about subject areas, information about occupations, working life, and educational and training routes.

Some of this material may be held in diverse places within the school or college. It will be important for planning partners to know where they may refer students and what is available for them. Such a database of in-house materials and mentors could be created by the development team.

The team may also consider how the careers library could be enhanced, given that the focus of much IAP work is on the period of transition. Effective partnerships with the Careers Service will ensure that this area of IAP work can be well supported. Reference to some of the following texts could also prove useful:

Careers Information in Schools and Colleges Guidelines (TEED)
Help Yourself: Setting Up and Running a Careers Library (COIC)
Careers Information and Careers Libraries: A Practical Guide (Trotman)

It is worthwhile noting that in order to meet the imperatives for enhanced careers education, documented in the White Paper *Education and Training for the Twenty-First Century*, financial assistance will be available through TECs to enhance the provision found in school and college careers libraries.

Some of the following texts and software are further sources of information for teaching staff and students. The list is by no means exhaustive nor recommended, it is simply a guide.

Reference books

Occupations (COIC)
Careers Guide (Cascaid)
Job File (Hodder and Stoughton)
A–Z of Careers and Jobs (Kogan Page)
Careers Opportunities for Everyone (Hobsons)
Careers Encyclopaedia (Cassell)
Job Outlines (COIC)
If I Were... (COIC)
Look at Work (COIC)
Working in Books (COIC)
Signposts Box (COIC)
Equal Opportunities Commission materials.

Assisting Transition

Choice at year 9
Your GCSE Decisions (Trotman)
Decisions 13/14 (Hobsons)
Which Way Now? (COIC)

Choice at year 11
Making a Choice at 16+ (Letts)
Decisions 15/16 (Hobsons)
It's Your Choice (COIC)
Your Choice of A Levels (Hobsons)
Focus at 16 (Newpoint: produced regionally)

Choice at 17/18
Making Decisions at 18+ (Letts)
Decisions 17/18 (Hobsons)
Jobs and Careers after A Levels (Hobsons)
Your Choice of Degree and Diploma (Hobsons)
The Job Book (Hobsons)

There may be additional locally produced information.

Education and Training

General information on further and higher education should be supplemented by prospectuses from colleges and universities, information from UCCA, PCAS and ADAR and information about student loans and grants.

More general guides include:

Which Degree (Newpoint)
Degree Course Guide Series (Hobsons)
Survey of HND Courses (Trotman)

Finally there should be information in formats other than text. Videos are available as is a range of computer software. Examples of the latter are:

- ECCTIS
- Jobfile Explorer
- Microdoors
- Kudos

The National Council for Education Technology (NCET) publishes '*The Careers Software Review*' which reviews software (North Yorkshire Youth Development Project, 1992b).

Developing Partnerships with Individuals and Agencies

Although it is to be hoped that the IAP development work was not launched into a void, it is likely that more detailed work with other individuals and agencies will come during the period of consolidation and expansion.

The Careers Service

The Careers Service may have been involved in early IAP planning work: certainly they should be involved as IAP expands. The Careers Service can help, as indicated earlier, with the development of a sound information base for young people to enable them to explore occupations and training routes. The Careers Service should be partnered by teaching staff so that careers education can be more systematically planned and integrated into young people's learning. It should, if possible, extend throughout young people's education and training.

The Careers Service need to be involved in IAP work to ensure that information which is collected about young people as they approach transition does not simply replicate information collected for the Careers

Service Summaries of Guidance. Working partnerships with Careers Officers should ensure they have access to Plans at transition. This will enable them to work more effectively with young people, building upon previously collected information.

Parents

Some parents may have been told about IAP work from the outset. It is clear from development work that parents can prove a useful source of support for young people, particularly in the early years of the process. Thus, during the consolidation and expansion stage teaching staff should review what they have told parents and be sure that they are fully informed of the IAP process, its potential outcomes, and the ways in which they may support young people. Parents can assist young people in reaching their targets and helping them monitor their progress. Parents can assist young people by becoming more informed about their education or training programme and by finding more out about the process of transition which their child faces.

Employers

During this stage, teaching staff should consider what they have told employers about IAP and either reinforce earlier messages or set about systematically informing employers. Employers will either be providers of work experience or be part-time employers of young people. Employers need to be aware that they can contribute to young people's personal and vocational development and to the realisation of targets on their Action Plans. Employers can also reinforce the school- or college-based IAP processes by constructing training plans with young people for their temporary period of employment.

Finally, some employers will be able to rehearse the long-term benefits of IAP work with young people. Some employers will themselves construct training plans with employees and undertake employee appraisal. Exploring with young people how these employment-based activities match and echo the IAP processes and Plans with which the young people have become familiar at school or college will lend status to IAP and encourage young people to appreciate that there can be long-term gains from early mastery of IAP processes.

As with the other areas of developing IAP work, the formation of partnerships with parents, the Careers Service and employers will require monitoring to determine how these agencies and individuals understand IAP, how well they engage with their own roles, and finally how they may be assisting young people with their targets.

Action planning partnerships can be illustrated as a web (Figure 7.1).

Figure 7.1 Individual Action Planning web

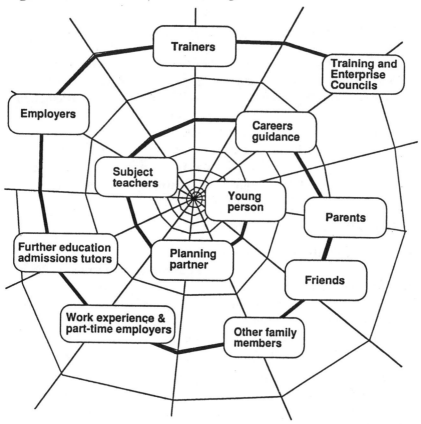

Stage IV: Developing Young People's Opportunities for Experiencing Coherence and Progression

One of the underlying reasons for IAP is to enhance young people's opportunities for experiencing coherence in their education, training and employment lives and thus to feel a sense of personal progression and development. This will be achievable if firstly IAP processes are integrated across the activities of the school or college which they attend. The second way in which coherence and progression might be achieved is through the creation of partnerships with those employers, educators and trainers who may receive young people. In part, the process of feeding young people's school- or college-based experiences of IAP into the receiving institution at transition, is formalised through the National

Record of Achievement.

However, employers, trainers or admissions tutors can gain more from young people having experienced IAP than simply having a document at transition. Employers, trainers and college or university admissions tutors need to be made aware of how they may work with young people, through the interview process, to tease out the young people's self-knowledge, the information and analysis on which they have based their decisions, and the ways in which they envision their immediate and longer-term futures. Employers, trainers and admissions tutors need to be trained to draw out and make use of the greater levels of self-awareness and articulateness which young people engaging with IAP will have gained.

Thus the development team needs to acquaint employers, trainers and admissions tutors with the IAP process and its likely outcomes, and to offer advice on ways to work with the information young people will have gathered. One starting point is the following cycle which has been proposed by the Essex-based Youth Development Project.

An Action Planning Cycle for Colleges

Activity A: Identify Existing Skills

During recruitment interviews staff will need to use existing documentation brought from school.

This may include information on the application form within the young person's Record of Achievement, of from reports and references.

During the interview further information may be provided by the student, possibly up-dating that which is written.

Activity B: Determine Goals

The Admissions Tutor, or similar post-holder, will support the young person in determining goals. These may be long term targets, such as identifying the appropriate course for the young person, the level within a programme of study or which 'A' levels are a suitable choice.

Activity C: Determine Learning Provision

The Course Tutor will explore the learning needs of the student early on in the programme.

Areas of weakness can be identified for additional support, and strengths can be acknowledged. Units of competence within NVQs can be detailed and clear programmes of study recorded.

Activity D: Determine Provision

Together, student and tutor will agree how, where and when the student will undertake the programme. This may include classroom based activity, open learning materials, supported self-study, and workshop sessions.

The final task of this phase of the Action Planning process is to agree on the best range of provision for the student.

Many students are becoming proficient in reviewing and planning during their Secondary Education, and providers of Post-16 education need to utilise the skills of these young people.

Employers and trainers need to be made aware that young people will have been engaged in developing skills such as:

- target setting;
- reviewing personal progress;
- thinking about personal and professional development;
- identifying strengths and weaknesses;
- identifying learning and development needs;
- thinking about routes to meeting such needs;
- self-presentation and self-advocacy;
- communication;
- negotiation;
- time management;
- prioritising.

These will help young people who join the workplace or training establishment to:

- discuss their progress objectively;
- jointly set new targets;
- understand appraisal processes.

It may mean that people skilled in IAP practices may become more motivated, focused, and more committed if they are able to realise their development needs.

So that these prospective benefits to employers, trainers and the individuals themselves are more than paper statements, the development teams, employers and trainers will have to work in concert. They need to determine:

- What is understood about RoA and IAP processes in the work and training place.
- What ways IAP and RoA are used at interview and for selection.
- What sorts of induction and training are offered to new entrants and the ways in which these might link with previously acquired skills in Action Planning.

- What types of career development discussions are open to new entrants.
- How appraisal operates.
- How IAP skills may link with these.

Until employers and trainers are exposed to IAP and forced to consider how such processes can be built upon, opportunities for effective progression at transition are jeopardised.

Conclusion

This chapter has considered the initiation and development of IAP within a single institution. The development of IAP has been considered in terms of several distinct phases, each of which has certain tasks which have to be undertaken. An emphasis has been placed throughout the chapter on the importance of senior management support, with its power to resource, place IAP on the timetable, and on the institution's Development Plan. Without such support, IAP will be based on insecure foundations.

The chapter has emphasised throughout the importance of testing the processes and documentation, looking for overlap and reinforcement within the curriculum and trying to rationalise paperwork and the type of information collected. The necessity for evaluation has been a feature of every stage of development work. The importance of integrating IAP processes throughout young people's experiences of the institution has been noted, as have the links with those agencies who receive young people. Without the creation of partnerships with colleagues within the school or college and with employers, trainers and colleges or university admissions tutors one of the crucial aims of IAP, that of enhancing young people's experiences of coherence and progression through enabling them to take greater and informed charge of their careers, will founder. Again the efficacy of such partnerships, the knowledge of IAP and the degree to which young people know how to and do approach others, needs to be evaluated.

Finally the chapter noted the importance of creating partnerships either through informing or actively working with agencies and individuals who might support young people or assist the development work. Parents, part-time employers and the Careers Service were in this category. Educators in schools and colleges developing IAP are to be encouraged to disseminate their work and gain external support. Just as IAP cannot be undertaken by a hero innovator, so it cannot be effected by an isolationist institution.

8 The Way Ahead

Introduction

At the close of this Guide to IAP there are the opportunities to draw together several issues explored within the text and to highlight areas for future work and consideration.

Several tenets of IAP

There are a number of keystones to successful IAP. It is hoped that this guide has explored these in such a way that they will be translatable into practice within a range of institutions.

The main messages about IAP are:

- the importance of the process and its dominance over the product;
- the importance of empowerment;
- the life-long benefits which accrue from acquiring the transferable skills of IAP;
- the significance of creating a fully informed and functioning IAP web;
- the importance of integrating IAP across the curriculum, within and beyond the institution.

The first three points above are interrelated. They concern the role and the experiences of the young person, and the climate which has to be created in order that quality IAP takes place.

Process over product

The process has innumerable benefits for young people. It is a means through which they gain undivided attention, expert help, information and referrals. It is an occasion when within their busy college or school lives they are asked to reflect on who they are, how they might like to make use of their skills and talents, and what they should like to do to explore and develop their potential. Undertaken well IAP can be an energising and exciting activity. IAP can be a positive experience, encouraging a justifiable sense of competence and confidence. IAP can be a time when aspirations gain the foundations to become workable options.

Transferable skills and life-long learning

The process has a range of important educative functions. Through encouragement, exemplar and discussion young people can acquire a range of skills essential to effective decision-making, to time and personal management and a number of keys to better self-understanding. Such skills and insights will stand them in good stead.

Similarly the experience of learning the processes of IAP will be valuable ones. The process can be taken into other learning arenas, into leisure time, into solving personal or social problems and addressing concerns. Stress is continually laid upon the importance of developing a nation of independent learners, of people who appreciate their own development and who gravitate towards ways of meeting their occupational and personal development needs. IAP certainly is a tool to enable this type of individual growth.

Empowerment

The time spent discussing personal selves, future options and strategies for development can free the imagination and thinking of some young people, who may then be emboldened to test the unknown. IAP teaches young people the importance of informed decision making and how to work towards it. Finally, IAP also liberates young people by ensuring that they have free access to plentiful information and advice.

Understanding and acquiring IAP as a series of skills, processes and routines for personal organisation have great benefits for the young person in the immediate and longer-term. Practising IAP with comprehension during school and college years equips the young adult for the assessment, appraisal and development processes which they will face in the adult worlds of education, training and employment.

Finally there are a cluster of key messages to be heeded about implementing IAP. These all relate to the importance of an integrated approach to developing and delivering IAP.

Integrating IAP across the curriculum, within and beyond the institution

Without a firm institutional base it will not be possible for any teaching staff to drive IAP forward. IAP has resource implications, for the document itself, staff training and setting aside time for Action Planning sessions. There are also institutional implications in developing appropriate policies to support IAP and the process of rationalising the assessment processes so that IAP can be integrated with other recording and assessment systems.

Creating a fully informed and functioning IAP web

The importance of developing a web of colleagues within the school or college is essential. Without shared understandings of the uses and value of IAP, it will not be consistently approached nor supported. As a result students may receive contradictory messages or become disheartened at the lack of help. Without communication networks teachers will themselves be isolated, each trying to function from within their own knowledge base and area of expertise. Without sharing information and qualities which their colleagues may have, staff will needlessly replicate effort and may offer overall, a weaker IAP experience to the young people in their care.

The institution needs to be corporately proactive, extending itself to ensure that its IAP work is supported by other professional agencies. There needs to be clear communication to parents and others, such as employers who may assist young people in achieving their IAP targets. While, for progression and coherence to be more than simple buzz-words the institution needs to work alongside those agencies, individuals and organisations which receive young people and their Action Plans. Without communicating 'up the line' there will be no understanding of the work which young people have undertaken to produce their Plan, nor any comprehension of the basis on which they rest their vocational or educational objectives. If the young person's strength of commitment to a particular course of action and the foundation for this commitment is not understood then there may be less effective matching between a young person's needs, interests, aims and abilities than there should have been.

Looking Forward

There are several areas where work remains to be undertaken. A few of which can be listed as:

- the role of end-users;
- the importance of a common technical language;
- the abolition of empires;
- the need to cultivate a culture which encourages training and personal development;
- ensuring that a written product does not dominate.

End-users, a common technical language and the creation of common interest

The first three of these points are interlinked. It is clear from the foregoing that communication has to be opened with those who may receive young people and their Action Plans. Without this end-users may not take notice of the Plan. Part of this process of communication needs to be the creation of a foundation of common understanding about the processes, products and longer-term outcomes. This will be facilitated by the creation of common definitions and a common language which will enable different agencies to talk to others outside their institutional parameter fences. Without such sharing and developing a common approach the work which is begun in one institution may not become the basis for the developmental work in another. This will cause frustration for the individual and be a waste of the human and other resources already expended in the processes of planning and creating a Plan.

The lack of a common language and understanding has other effects. It also ensures that individuals may remain isolated within their own spheres of developmental work or within what they feel to be their own interests or areas of expertise. This can lead to a continuing situation in which areas of expertise or knowledge are colonised, and interests, either personal or institutional are fortified. This does not encourage communication or the integration which is deemed so essential for the effective delivery and development of IAP.

Without common language and understanding there will also be a failure to understand the roles which each agency may play and the attributes which can be brought to a developing IAP.

Cultivating a culture which encourages training and personal development

With a common approach to IAP and sharing an understanding of personal and occupational development will come momentum for the development of the culture of training which so many of the policy-makers, trainers and employers espouse as vital to national and individual well-being. Without the commitment to vocational learning it is likely that the move to develop IAP as a vehicle of life-long learning will meet many barriers and constraints. Individual's reasons for wanting professional or personal development may be questioned and particular goals may be re-routed to meet the imperatives of the work-place. If IAP is to develop then the vocational climate and culture will have to fall into step with the rhetoric of employers and politicians.

Ensuring that a written product does not dominate

There are concerns that the process may become subsumed in the production of an Action Plan. The crux of this problem lies in the way in which

Action Plans may be used. If there is a move to accredit completed Action Plans then this would shift the emphasis away from formative and working materials open to revision, and towards a clear series of objectives to be met.

Similarly if Action Plans are the means to release funds for training and guidance then there will be a heavy emphasis on completing the document. If funded courses of action are tied to the Plans, then again there may well be fewer opportunities for changing course and reconsidering Plans. If the completion of Action Plans themselves are the means by which the guidance workers are paid, then this again shifts the emphasis from process to production.

Should the Plan come to dominate for any of these or indeed any other reasons, then it is possible that those tutoring staff not directly involved in such processes will move away from IAP believing that the work is undertaken by others with a specific remit. If this were to happen then it would be to the detriment of students who would loose the immediate gains from protracted IAP processes and they would have fewer opportunities to cultivate the various transferable IAP skills.

It is to be hoped that the product does not dominate but that IAP processes become entrenched within the educational lives of young people.

> ...this country is unlikely to have a fully effective learning system for young people in the labour market unless that system becomes more self sustaining –'built into the furniture'. (Young people) ... need to be more aware of the value of continued learning and how to set about securing it. Without this commitment to learning, and knowledge of how to work the system, vocational education and training will continue to be regarded by many as something that is 'done to them' rather than their own opportunity for development and reward.
>
> (Department of Employment, 1990)

Appendix

Action
Planning

Bexley
LONDON BOROUGH

BEXLEY ADVISORY SERVICE

ACTION PLANNING
YEAR 9 INFORMATION BOOKLET

DESIGNED BY THE PUPILS OF BLACKFEN SCHOOL ACTION PLANNING
PROJECT COHORT
(under direction of Mrs June Lloyd, Careers Teacher)

BEXLEY LONDON BOROUGH
DIRECTORATE OF EDUCATION
© Crown Copyright May 1991

What is Action Planning?

Action Planning helps you to focus on your future and your interests.

Action Planning makes you think of yourself in a different way.

It does this by helping you to identify long and short term goals that are connected with your interests and/or the job you want to do.

These goals must be achievable and achieved within a time plan, for this you plan carefully and should be confident that you can succeed.

While you are trying to plan your future you will gradually find out your weaknesses and your strengths but you must remember to plan each step carefully.

One of the best things about **Action Planning** is that you can stop and review your progress.

You can set yourself new, short term goals as you achieve each of the previous ones.

You can even change your long term goal as you grow and develop.

How we began Action Planning

My Careers Teacher/Tutor explained what is meant by **Action Planning**, once I really understood what I was going to do, I was given a self assessment pack to complete.

This consisted of some sheets about my interests, my talents, strengths and weaknesses. The exercise really made me think about myself. Once I had finished the pack I realised that I knew quite a lot about myself.

In our groups we talked about ourselves, our interests, our strengths and our weaknesses and then we wrote our first **Action Plan**. We set ourselves short term and long term goals.

I knew that I needed to improve my spelling and work harder at my French. These were two of my short term goals.

I can change my goals or my whole future plan each time that I review my **Action Plan**.

My Teacher/Tutor explained that the piece of paper, the **Action Paper** was written on, was not half as important as my thoughts and plans, that made me think about myself.

I feel that since I started **Action Planning** I look at myself in a different way, I am trying now to build on my own strengths and improve upon my weaknesses.

The unbroken circle of Planning and Achievement

This circle shows how **Action Planning** fits into the Record of Achievement.

The Record of Achievement shows what we have accomplished to date and the **Action Planning** charts show where we hope to go in the future.

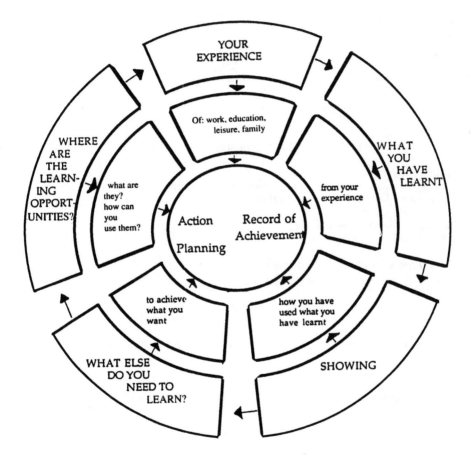

130

Here is an example of an **Action Plan** to help you when writing your own plan (only the names have been changed)

School   Hillview

NAME R K Patel   Date Spring Term

MY LONG TERM AIM IS: Engineering

The education/training route to this is:

1 GCSE's

2 Job with training

3 Youth Training

4 Gain promotion in a job

To reach this I need to take the following steps:	Timescale
1 Choose my option choice carefully by getting advice from my Teacher and reading the information in the Careers Library	by end of next month
2 Try harder in my science subjects by asking more questions in class	by NOW
3 Spend more time on my homework check my homework for spelling mistakes	by NOW
4 Design a gadget for collecting litter as part of my project	by half term
5 Complete my model kit	by end of next week
6	by
I will review this on:	end of the term
Student R K Patel	Reviewer: Tutor

Here is an example of an **Action Plan** to help you when writing your own plan (only the names have been changed)

School   Hillview

NAME H Smith   Date Spring Term

MY LONG TERM AIM IS: to work in a Bank as a
                                                 Bank Clerk

The education/training route to this is:

1 GCSE's

2 "A" levels

3 Job in a Bank

4 Banking exams:

To reach this I need to take the following steps: Timescale

1 Try harder in Maths by answering more
  questions in the class and asking if I don't   by NOW
  understand

2 Read the information about Banking in the   by HALF TERM
  Careers Library

3 Make sure my homework is in on time   by NOW

4 Choose Information Technology as
  one of my options   by by two weeks time

5 Volunteer to be the Treasurer at the Youth   by next week
  Club

6 Read at least one book a week and join   by at the weekend
  the local library

I will review this on: end of the term

Student H Smith   Reviewer: Tutor

                                                    (ref JB/APP Yr 9 Booklet)

References

Crichton, L. (1989) *Developing Personal Effectiveness*, Sheffield: COIC.

Department of Employment (1990) *The Skills Decade*, Sheffield: TEED.

Hargreaves, R. and Reynolds, D. (eds) (1989) *Education Policies: Controversies and Critiques*, Lewes: Falmer Press.

North Yorkshire Youth Development Project (1992a) *Models of Individual Action Planning*, York Careers Service.

North Yorkshire Youth Development Project (1992b) *Models of Individual Action Planning for Schools*, York Careers Service.

Radnor, H. (1992) *The Problems in Facilitating Qualitative Formative Assessment in Pupils*, Stirling: British Educational Research Association research paper.

Squirrell, G. (1991) *Individual Action Planning: Development Work with 14–17 Year Olds*, Bristol: Centre for Assessment Studies, University of Bristol.

Squirrell, G. (1992a) *Report on the Youth Development Project Initiative*, Sheffield: Careers Occupation Information Service.

Watts, A.G. (1991) Individual action planning: issues and strategies. *British Journal of Work and Education*, **5 (1)**, 47–63.

Further Reading

CBI (1990) *Towards a Skills Revolution*, London: CBI.

Cleaton, D. (1993) *Social and Personal Education*, London: Careers Consultants Ltd.

Crichton, L. (1989) *Developing Personal Effectiveness*, Sheffield: COIC.

DES (1991) *Education and Training for the 21st Century*, London: HMSO.

Egan, G. (1986) *The Skilled Helper 3rd edition*, California: Brooks Cole Publishing Co.

Department of Employment (1990) *The Skills Decade*, Sheffield: TEED.

Department of Employment (1991) *A Strategy for Skills*, London: Employment Department.

Hargreaves, R. and Reynolds, D. (eds) (1989) *Education Policies: Controversies and Critiques*, Lewes: Falmer Press.

Hopson, B. and Scally, M. (1980) *Life Skills Teaching Programmes No 1*, Leeds: Lifeskills Associates.

Hopson, B. and Scally, M. (1982) *Life Skills Teaching Programmes No 2*, Leeds: Lifeskills Associates.

Hopson, B. and Scally, M. (1982) *Life Skills Teaching Programmes No 3*, Leeds: Lifeskills Associates.

Hopson, B. and Scally, M. (1988) *Life Skills Teaching Programmes No 4*, Leeds: Lifeskills Associates.

Hopson, B. and Scally, M. (1991) *Build Your Own Rainbow*, London: Mercury Business Paperbacks.

Millar, R., Crute, V. and Hargie, O. (1992) *Professional Interviewing*, London: Routledge and Kegan Paul.

North Yorkshire Youth Development Project (1992a) *Models of Individual Action Planning*, York: Careers Service.

North Yorkshire Youth Development Project (1992b) *Models of Individual Action Planning for Schools*, York: Careers Service.

Radnor, H. (1992) *The Problems in Facilitating Qualitative Formative Assessment in Pupils*, Stirling: British Educational Research Association research paper.

Squirrell, G. (1991) *Individual Action Planning: Development Work with*

14–17 Year Olds, Bristol: Centre for Assessment Studies, University of Bristol.

Squirrell, G. (1992a) *Report on the Youth Development Project Initiative*, Sheffield: Careers Occupation Information Service

Squirrell, G. (1992b) *Guide to Developing Individual Action Planning*, London South Thames: Training and Enterprise Council.

Squirrell, G. (1992c) *Guide to Developing Individual Action Planning in Schools and Colleges*, London South Thames: Training and Enterprise Council.

TEED (1991) *Assessment, Guidance and Action Planning, Developing Good Practice Series*, available through TEED, Moorfoot, Sheffield.

Tunstall, P. *et al.* (1992) *London Individual Action Planning Project*, London: University of London, Institute of Education.

Watts, A.G. (1991) Individual action planning: issues and strategies. *British Journal of Work and Education*, **5 (1)**, 47–63.

Index